How to Become a
Successful
Manager

by
Gerard Assey

Published by:

F-2/16, Ansari road, Daryaganj, New Delhi-110002
☎ 23240026, 23240027 • *Fax:* 011-23240028
Email: info@vspublishers.com • *Website:* www.vspublishers.com

Regional Office : Hyderabad
5-1-707/1, Brij Bhawan (Beside Central Bank of India Lane)
Bank Street, Koti, Hyderabad - 500 095
☎ 040-24737290
E-mail: vspublishershyd@gmail.com

Branch Office : Mumbai
☎ 022-23510736
E-mail vspublishersmum@gmail.com

Follow us on:

All books available at **www.vspublishers.com**

© **Copyright:** V&S PUBLISHERS
ISBN 978-93-813845-4-1

This book was earlier printed in the name of *Bite-sized bits on Common-sense Management*

The Copyright of this book, as well as all matter contained herein (including illustrations) rests with the Publisher. No person shall copy the name of the book, its title design, matter and illustrations in any form and in any language, totally or partially or in any form. Anybody doing so shall face legal action and will be responsible for damages.

Printed at : Param Offseters Okhla New Delhi-110020

Dedication & Appreciation

My very first book is firstly dedicated to the Glory of God – our Provider!

Next to my wife June (Bug!) – a constant source of inspiration – who persistently nagged me to get the manuscript completed. She 'visioned' me on 'press meets' and 'book release' functions.

To my two obedient, loving and hardworking children, Amanda and Roque, who were at most times deprived of my love and attention due to my late working or travel schedules.

To my loving and always cheerful mum ('Del', who brought us up so well) for assisting in the editing and proofreading.

To Sister Priscilla, for constantly upholding us in prayer.

To the staff of 'Collection Skills', who have had confidence in me and share my vision.

And, finally, to all the managers who worked with me some time or the other (in my years of experience of leading, controlling and interacting) from whom I have had the good fortune of being able to observe and painfully learn from the school of experience.

My sincere thanks to each one of you!

Dedicatedly yours,
Gerard

Contents

Introduction 7

Managing Your Basic Resource 9

Goal Setting for Success! 13

Interviewing and Selecting Sales Personnel 18

Training – An Investment 24

24 Rules for Training Meetings 28

Winning Your Way in Selling! 31

Telemarketing: Power of the Phone 34

How and When to Conduct Sales Meetings 38

Managing Bad Debt: The Importance of
    Good Cash Collection Skills 42

Caring for Your Customer – Part I 44

Caring for Your Customer – Part II 47

32 Ways to Motivate Your Sales Team
    – And Yourself! 50

Ongoing Coaching for Sales Personnel 55

Effective Communication Skills 64

The Skills of Problem Solving 74

Delegation: A Manager's Greatest Attribute 78

The Importance of Good Human Relations 81

Self-development 84

Afterword 99

Introduction

In most organisations, very often, top sales performers are moved up to the sales management position without evaluating whether they have the required skills to perform the tasks of a manager. The sales manager's position is seen as a reward for the outstanding sales performer. But the person in question may or may not have the aptitude to be a manager, as the qualities required for a sales manager are definitely different from those required for a successful salesperson. *An outstanding salesperson need not necessarily evolve into an outstanding sales manager!*

As a consequence, the newly promoted manager is unable to cope with this transition from working independently to that of now handling a team. The saddest part is that the newly promoted manager has not been provided with any training whatsoever, but has just been moved up and asked to function from the very moment he assumes this new role.

In the process, the organisation has not only lost their top salesperson but also acquired a poor sales manager with this person eventually not doing justice to that position. This results in a build up of low morale and attrition all around, thus affecting productivity, tarnishing the company's image and eventually ending in frustration for all.

In my years of experience of leading, controlling and interacting with several hundreds of salesmen and sales managers, I have had the good fortune of being able to observe and painfully learn from first-hand experience how these managers failed because of this lack of training.

Therefore, to some extent, this book should be able empower the newly promoted manager with the various aspects of management applicable to any type of organisation, regardless of the product or service (with more emphasis on ongoing coaching skills… the most important function of a sales manager). Small in size, but packed with powerful, practical insights, each chapter is independent and easy to read.

An invaluable resource for the newly promoted sales manager… his/her first kit!

ooo

Managing Your Basic Resource

Imagine a situation where you are given Rs.86,400 and told: "From this moment, you have 24 hours to invest this amount. You can invest in anything you want to with this money. Whatever you don't invest, I get back tomorrow at this exact moment."

What would you do in the next 24 hours? You'd be working hard and fast to invest that Rs.86,400 – wouldn't you?! That being our attitude, why aren't we busily investing as much as we can of the 86,400 seconds given to us everyday? Yes, at the beginning of each day we are all given 86,400 seconds and as each one ticks by, we have lost it forever, unless we find a way to invest that moment in the future.

Most of us waste about half our time. Most wasted time is due to poor habits and lack of self-discipline. How do you then acquire good habits and self-discipline? Managing time is really a matter of managing your own behaviour. To change this behaviour you need to create a reward system that rewards productive behaviour and discourages time wasting. Good time management is making first-rate habits second nature. Remember, "Until you can manage yourself, you can't manage anything else".

Before you begin, however, have a set of clear written goals that you wish to accomplish and have them ranked in order of importance.

Next, take a one-week time inventory, as we may not be aware of most of our habits until we make a conscious effort to discover them. Taking a hard, objective look at your own behaviour is one of the best favours you could do yourself. You can't replace bad habits with good ones until you identify the former. Write down everything you do for one week on a DAILY TIME LOG form (Fig 1), starting each day with your name, the day and date. Be sure to list every activity and why it occurred, rating each activity for its importance and urgency (e.g., for very urgent, write A1; for medium priority or not urgent, write B3), whether planned (P) or an interruption (I). When you finish working on one activity or an interruption, write down the amount of time used.

Daily Time Log

Name .... Day .... Date ....

Starting Time	Activity	Imp./ Urg.	Plan./ Int.	Time Used	Comments

Figure 1

Importance
A. Top priority (must do)
B. Medium priority (should do)
C. Low priority

Urgency
1. Must be done now
2. Should be done soon
3. Not urgent

At the end of the week take an inventory, noting the kinds of activities that occur most frequently, like phone calls, interacting with customers, visitors, paperwork, meetings, socialising etc. Summarise the week by writing down each major category of time used and the percentage of total time consumed. Now you know where your time is going! Chances are it isn't going where you thought it was! But don't get discouraged. Even the best people waste around two hours a day!

Now, honestly write the answers to these questions:
1. What are my greatest time-wasters?
2. How much time is consumed by interruptions? Who or what is most responsible for them? How can this be reduced?
3. Am I doing tasks that are unimportant? How can this be reduced, eliminated or delegated?
4. Whom do I need to see more or less often?
5. What activities need more time?
6. What activities need less time?
7. Am I trying to do too much?
8. Am I procrastinating?
9. What habits or tendencies are causing me to waste time?

When you have made your time-inventory statement and answered the questions, treat yourself to a nice reward for having the courage to discover your own weaknesses. It's a tough exercise but one that will pay big dividends. Once you have recognised your faults or time-wasters, it takes about three weeks to transform a new way of behaving into a comfortable habit. Most people fail to realise this. Instead, they try to make radical, wholesale changes in their behaviour, find it unbearable and go back to their old, comfortable habits. The key to making lasting changes in your behaviour is to make them gradually, smoothly and systematically.

Review your time-inventory questions. Now choose one new habit that you feel will have the greatest timesaving value and resolve to practise it for three weeks without fail. Once you decide on a new habit, announce the change to everyone and start practising it immediately, while deciding a reward you can give yourself after three weeks of consistent success at practising the new habit. This will be your incentive to practise the new behaviour until it becomes second nature. The reward for your success and self-discipline need not be enormous, but it must be meaningful.

Bear in mind: every good, new habit you acquire has in-built rewards for more free time, less stress and higher productivity with long-term payoffs. You are gaining the skills that turn talent into ability.

After you unfailingly practise a new behaviour for three weeks, it will probably become a well-entrenched habit. So give yourself that reward and choose another new habit (and reward!) to practise for the next three weeks. Keep repeating the self-management cycle and over a period of months you will begin to see drastic and lasting improvements in your productivity.

Simultaneously, decide daily what goals and activities are most important, as they would have become obvious after the exercise. Eliminate low-priority items. Ritually prepare a TO DO LIST (Fig 2) for the following day and rank your goals/activities in terms of URGENT, HIGH, MEDIUM and LOW.

Begin each day with a definite plan referring to this TO DO LIST. Develop your own systems so that you do not waste time shuffling paper (bills, memo's etc). And do not worry about what was not completed – you cannot fix something that is past!

To Do List				
ACTIVITY/GOAL	PRIORITY			
	U	H	M	L
CONCENTRATE ON HIGH PRIORITY & URGENT ITEMS FIRST				
U-URGENT M-MEDIUM PRIORITY H-HIGH PRIORITY L-LOW PRIORITY				

Figure 2

Lastly, we must all learn to work smart. Talking about working smart, I'm reminded of the story Dale Carnegie once narrated. Two men were out chopping wood. One man worked hard all day, took no breaks and only stopped briefly for lunch. The other chopper took several breaks and a short nap at lunch. At the end of the day, the man who had taken no breaks was quite disturbed to see that the other had cut more wood than he had. He said, "I don't understand. Every time I looked around, you were sitting down, yet you cut more wood than I did."

His companion remarked, "Did you also notice that while sitting down, I was sharpening my axe?!"

Use your time wisely – work smart!

Goal Setting for Success!

| Before you score, you must first have a goal. |

Years ago, advertising legend David Ogilvy set out to establish a great advertising agency within a dozen years. At that time, he was a small tobacco farmer in Pennsylvania. On his second day of business, he made a list of five clients he most wanted to get. They were Bristol-Myers, Campbell Soup, General Foods, Lever Brothers and Shell Oil Company. Eventually, he had them all. The quickest way, therefore, to get what you want is to **identify** what you want.

Establishing attainable goals and being motivated enough is certainly not an easy task but a necessary one that can be done with the proper means. But we must remember that establishing unreasonable or impossible goals and standards will in most cases have a detrimental effect.

Certain criteria need to be borne in mind for effective goal setting:

1. **Is it worthwhile?** Do you desire the benefits strongly enough to make you determined to achieve it?

2. **Is it achievable?** Although it shouldn't be a "piece of cake", it must be hard enough to demand the use of your talents.
3. **Is it well defined?** Do you know exactly what is to be achieved?
4. **What are the obstacles?** Have they all been considered?
5. **Is it measurable?** Can the progress of the goal be measured?
6. **Are workable increments possible?** Can the major goal be split into minor ones?

To get people excited about a hobby, career, job or any activity, the task must normally have four key ingredients:

1. A meaningful goal.
2. A way to keep score, so people can see and measure their progress.
3. Control over achieving the goal.
4. Meaningful rewards.

Step 1: Choose the Results You Want

Good management always starts with solid, specific, written goals. Sit down with each person (or group, if it's a group goal) and decide, in precise terms, what key results are to be achieved by a specific date.

To help people set good goals, follow these guidelines:

- The group's goals should help you achieve your goals and must contribute to the achievement of company goals. Show them your goals and the company's goals and ask, "How can you help?"
- Ensure their goals are stated in terms of results to be achieved, not activities to be performed. For example, making more phone calls is an activity. Increasing sales revenue by 20 per cent in the next six months is a result.
- State goals briefly and write them down. This helps increase clarity and commitment.
- When you can, let people set their own goals. Self-set goals are more meaningful. But if people want you to set goals for them, do it. What matters most is that everyone understands what has to be done.
- Set only a few goals for each person or group and rank them in order of importance. More than two or three goals end up becoming no goals!
- Check goals for compatibility, so that the achievement of one does not preclude achieving another.
- Goals that are challenging but attainable get the best performance.

Encourage people to choose battles big enough to matter but small enough to win.

One of the most crucial things to remember about goals is: *People are willing to do what can be measured.* This makes it imperative that every major goal has a scoring system that reflects the results you are trying to achieve.

Don't fall for the classic line: "You can't measure what I do." If the performance of a person or group can't be measured, chances are they aren't contributing much. In deciding how to measure, keep these points in mind:

- *Keep the system simple.* Use only one or two measures for each goal. Otherwise, people will spend too much time measuring and too little doing!
- *Measure outputs instead of activities.* Performance measure should indicate progress towards results achieved. For example, here are some common performance measures for different departments: **Sales:** Rupees of sales. **Accounts:** Number of vouchers processed. **Maintenance:** Number of work orders completed.

The best measures give people frequent feedback so they can monitor their performance and adapt accordingly.

It is most important to measure group goals than to measure individual goals. Team performance counts the most.

Step 2: Identify the Behaviour Needed

It is important for people to know and understand their goals. But they cannot <u>do</u> a goal so the next step is to identify the kinds of behaviour most crucial to achieving a given goal. To identify the necessary behaviours, choose the kinds of behaviour you feel are most crucial to achieving the goal. Rank them in order of importance and write them down.

Ask those responsible for achieving the goal to do the same thing without having seen your choices. Meet and reach a joint agreement on what kinds of behaviour are most important for successfully achieving this goal.

Step 3: Decide on the Proper Rewards

As you read this, you may be thinking: "Ho-hum! Set goals. Write them down. I've tried it before and it doesn't work. It's just a waste of time, paper and money."

The reason so many goal-setting programmes fail is that the goals are not directly linked to specific rewards. Good goals only start people moving in the right direction. You need specific rewards to keep them moving. Trying to get results without rewards is like trying to run an engine without fuel. Remember: the right rewards for the right behaviour gets the right results.

With so many ways to reward people, you may ask, "How do I decide how to reward each person?" The answer is simple: Ask them! Everyone will attach different values to a given reward. So when you sit down to identify goals, take extra time to set specific rewards. Make a list of possible rewards and let people choose one or combine several. But ensure the rewards are specifically spelled out and are proportional to the importance of the goal. For group goals, be sure that each individual knows how he will be rewarded when the group achieves the goals.

Step 4: Use the Power of Positive Feedback

Assume you have done everything discussed so far – set goals, identified the important behaviours to achieve the goals and chosen rewards. All you have to do now is sit back and reward people as they achieve their goals right? Not quite! There is a more crucial piece to the puzzle – positive feedback.

Achieving a major goal can take weeks, months or even years, and people need frequent reinforcement to keep them excited and encouraged. The way to keep people enthusiastic and on target is through positive feedback. Look for the good in people and let them know you value them. Make a special effort to recognise and praise good behaviour and you'll soon see that good behaviour being repeated. As Robert McNamara put it, "Brains, like hearts, go where they are appreciated."

In Step 2, you identified the most important kinds of behaviour necessary to achieve a major goal. This was to ensure a plan for knowing what kinds of behaviour to reward with positive feedback.

For positive feedback to work, your message should follow these guidelines:

- Personalise it for the individual.
- Deliver it on the spot, as soon as you see the good behaviour.
- Be sincere. Glad-handing and flattery won't work. People know when they are being conned.
- Be specific. When you see good behaviour, don't say: "Great job" or "Keep up the good work". Rather, word your message this way: "Rohan, how do you do it? It's the third contract you have landed this month. It's people like you who make all of us look good and I want you to know how much we all appreciate and need

you. It's so nice to be working with such a good performer and a great person."

There is another crucial guideline to remember about giving positive feedback. **Do it inconsistently**. That's right, inconsistently! Behaviour that is randomly reinforced is more likely to become habitual. It's much like gambling. A person knows the payoff is going to come but doesn't know when. So he keeps on trying! When you get the right results the final step is obvious.

Step 5: Dispense Rewards, Enjoy Success and Set New Goals

This is the easy, fun part of the job. Unfortunately, you may not always get the right results. In that case, your task is to sit down with the achiever(s) and try to decide what went wrong and how to fix it.

Are the goals correct and meaningful? Did everyone responsible understand them? Did you choose the right kinds of behaviour to reinforce? Are the rewards appropriate and meaningful? Did you give frequent positive feedback? Did outside forces make achieving the goal impossible? If so, what were they? What has to be changed to make success possible? Focus on problem solving and don't apportion blame or allow anyone else to do so. Tell all that their efforts are appreciated and point out the things they did well. Then get down to the business of finding out what went wrong, fix it and try again.

When Steve Jobs, founder of Apple Computer, was *twelve* years old, he called Bill Hewlett, founder of Hewlett-Packard and asked if they would give him some parts.

People who know where they are going know how to get there!

ooo

Interviewing and Selecting Sales Personnel

One of the most common mistakes many managers make is to undertake recruitment in haste. There is probably no other aspect of a manager's job that has more importance in long-term effects than the decision on whom to hire. Managers who choose not to "pay me now" (those who decide they don't have the time needed to interview thoroughly) will be those who end up "paying later" – in lost sales, low productivity, training time and extra work for themselves, not to mention carrying dead wood on their pay roles. They then become part of an ongoing cycle because they are so busy trying to keep their new recruit "up", the next time they need to interview again they don't have the time and make a quick hire and the cycle repeats itself.

One must therefore take time to thoroughly interview a candidate to ensure the "match" between the new recruit and the company is as close as one can get. This would call for sufficient advance planning.

Plan in Advance

The type and number of candidates required, outlining dates for recruitment advertisement(s), deadline for receipt of applications (if not a walk-in ad), date for call letters, initial interviews, second interviews (if required), at this stage keeping a good 50 per cent or more as standby (in case of dropouts before the final selection), final interviews and, lastly, induction into the company.

Planning

1. Decide on the type and number of candidates required.
2. Set dates for:
   - (a) Recruitment advertisement.

     (OR)

     Display notices at reputed colleges (best time, around the exams in March).
   - (b) Deadline for receipt of applications (if not walk-in).
   - (c) Despatch of letters.
   - (d) Initial interviews.
   - (e) Second interviews (if required).
   - (f) Final interviews.
   - (g) Induction into company.

Interview Process

This could be drawn up into three stages spread out on different dates (which gives you a chance to really assess or test how interested the candidate is in obtaining the job).

1. Initial interview or screening process.
2. The second interview – sales ability (only if necessary).
3. The final interview.

Initial Interview

- (a) Application form, if any, to be filled in. (Do not let the resume influence your opinion. There is usually more – or less! – to a person than you will find on this sheet of paper.) Do remember, everybody looks good on paper!
- (b) If required, conduct an aptitude test tailor-made to company needs to check on:
  1. Handwriting
  2. Alertness/sharpness
  3. Basic figure work (arithmetic)
  4. Spelling

(c) Overall, the interview process will consist of the following areas:
1. Impression (dress, personal grooming, posture, handshake, punctuality etc. If he doesn't look presentable or turn up on time for an interview, he won't do any better when he shows for the job.)
2. Background (family, recommendations, education, social and extracurricular activities, references etc.).
3. Attitude (towards life in general, people, work, etc.).
4. Communication skills.
5. Potential selling ability.
6. Compatibility with company culture/environment.
7. Future prospects – leadership potential.

(d) Personal interview with manager: (application form and aptitude test results with manager at this stage). Some points a manager needs to keep in mind:
- Review the application before the interview.
- Have an open, proper frame of mind.
- Give the candidate your undivided attention.
- Eliminate calls or interruptions. It's an important decision.
- Ensure the candidate does more talking than you do.
- Remember, you are interviewing him, not the other way around!
- Know what questions to ask – if you don't, the candidate may end up interviewing you!
- Make sure the candidate knows who you and others on the panel are – including names and titles.
- Speak slowly and clearly – it is a high-stress situation for the candidate and he may miss certain words.
- Use the candidate's name often and early.
- Smile – or a nervous candidate may not be able to showcase his good points.
- Start with easy questions to make the candidate comfortable and save the probing ones for later.

Follow a particular sequence, running through the details from the beginning to the end of the application (e.g. getting the candidate to begin with details of himself and his family background).

Check for:
- Incomplete sections (probe here).
- Missing or conflicting information.
- Any scratched, erased or overwritten entries.
- Gaps in employment or education.
- Reasons for leaving past employers. (Does he speak well of or criticises past employers? If he only voices criticism, he will probably be that way always – attitude problem!)
- Has he progressively moved up/had a steady growth in position/income?
- Glowing descriptions of accomplishments and titles (probe here to ensure they are not grossly exaggerated, meaningless or fancy titles – check duties in each job).

Education
- Why did he take up this course?
- What did he have in mind when taking up this course/degree?
- How does the candidate see his joining the company contributing to his career (especially in sales)?

Extracurricular
- Other than studies, what else was the candidate interested in at school/college?
- What sort of activities did he take part in?
- What was his role?
- Is he a loner or does he love working as part of a team?
- Is he a self-starter or does he need specific orders?
- What about his organising capabilities?
- Leadership – did he have a chance to lead a team?
- What did he feel about people in his team?
- Is he willing to take risks/challenges or participate in competitive events?
- Is he willing to learn new things?
- Finally, check for self-confidence.

Job
- How did he get this job (check whether most of his jobs were via influence or through merit)?

- How does he like the job?
- What made him leave his previous job? (Check his attitude.)
- If currently unemployed, why did he leave previous job before securing another one. (Were his services terminated? Why? Did he have a tiff with boss/colleague? Check past records on how and why he left the job.)
- What does he feel about his supervisor, boss or subordinate?
- What was his major contribution in the last job?
- What does he consider his greatest asset?
- What is it that interests the candidate about the new job or company?
- What does the candidate know about the company?
- How does the candidate visualise himself a couple of years from now?

Interview II (only if necessary)

Sales ability: Hold a mock session for the candidate to sell any product (e.g. an expensive pen or watch etc.). Check his control and presentation skills, including the ability to bounce back (resilience) when confronted with an objection.

Final Interview

By this stage, one would have had a fair chance to assess all short-listed candidates and would now have to decide on the best (depending on the requirement).

Other areas to check before investing time and money in training candidates:

1. Check if the candidate has a good number of close relatives (brothers/sisters/father/mother) abroad or a history of family business. (The chances are a candidate may not last for too long – so probe!)
2. Check for drug addiction or alcoholism (a difficult but important check). Red eyes with slurred speech could be an indicator, though difficult to assess, as positive signs start showing up only after couple of months of working. If in doubt, do not recruit at all. You may land up with a problem that could possibly spread.
3. Professionals like CAs, engineers or MBAs might seem interested, but may not last. They are only looking for a couple of years' experience before they settle into their own field.

4. Check to ensure candidate has a valid driving licence and/or a two-wheeler, if the position so demands.
5. Check on willingness to stay late after office hours (especially in case of girls), which is sometimes required.
6. Check on flexibility and willingness to move, if transferred (home commitments may preclude this).
7. If unmarried (for ladies) probe on plans for the future. Would the candidate continue working after marriage? If recently married, does the candidate have plans of starting a family in the near future (might affect a pre-planned schedule)?
8. Check on languages known (might be of use later). Experience shows that a candidate without selling experience is much easier to mould in the company's way of thinking than a candidate with experience (this should not be treated as a ground rule).

Conclusion

Invest all your time in such an exercise, as the recruitment process could ultimately affect your earnings and day-to-day activities. So give it all the time it deserves. Look at everyone you select today as a potential or future manager.

While placing a Russian doll before each director's chair, legendary adman and founder of Ogilvy & Mather, David Ogilvy told them, "That's you. Open it." On opening the doll, they found another one inside and another one inside it. Inside the smallest doll was a note: *"If you always hire people who are smaller than you are, we shall become a company of dwarfs. If, on the other hand, you always hire people who are bigger than you are, we shall become a company of giants."*

ooo

Training – An Investment

"If you wish to plan for a year – sow seeds; if you wish to plan for ten years – plant trees; if you wish to plan for a lifetime – develop a man," proclaims a famous Chinese proverb, highlighting the importance of training and development.

The socio-economic environment of India is changing fast. Economic liberalisation has led to competitiveness and globalisation, bringing in quick technological changes. This is forcing almost all companies to reconsider traditional strategies, policies and routine methods of doing business.

To keep up with environmental dynamics, organisations seek to change fast, but it is people within who bring about all changes. How they perform will determine how well the company copes with today's business environment.

Good training can contribute to behavioural change in people, thus affecting the desired changes in the organisation as a whole. When the changed organisation interacts with its environment, a new set of complications arise, which requires further change or adjustment of its people via retraining. This is a continuous process. However, organisations need to stretch beyond this reactive approach to the development function, which should form part of an organisation's corporate strategy, requiring the management's total commitment.

The message is clear. People must accelerate their development to make the required changes or face the possibility of being left behind. While ongoing education and development of potential skills and talents were once considered a luxury, today they are an absolute necessity.

Investment in quality training and development is therefore key to ensuring enhancement of staff performance and productivity in a fast-changing business scenario.

What exactly do we mean by training? The simplest definition for many is that training helps people learn. In reality, training should be the development and delivery of information that people will **apply** after learning, towards the goals of skill development and performance improvement. This definition distinguishes training from other methods of learning, where people are provided with information, but not necessarily expected to use it. Training will be an absolute failure if its fails to achieve its primary function – providing new knowledge, enhancing skills and/or changing attitudes and behaviour.

Identifying or assessing this training need – the gap between the knowledge, skills and attitudes required in a job and the knowledge, skills and attitude of the person carrying out the job – is the starting point of all training.

The training need could arise for many reasons, including:
- Change in culture, place or environment
- Change in people or posts
- Change in technology
- Growth or reduction in organisation
- Change in job or responsibilities

This training need will fall into one of four areas:

(a) **Job Training:** Training to give an employee the basic knowledge, skills and attitudes to carry out a task.

(b) **Performance Improvement:** Training to improve on current satisfactory performance or to overcome identified weakness in the current job.

(c) **Individual Development:** Training to add to, or develop, knowledge, skills and attitudes for a different job (at a higher level or a different job at the same level).

(d) **Change Training:** Training to cope with expected changes, e.g., changes in the organisation, products, processes, policies, procedures or methods.

However, assessing this need is one of the most vital areas in the training process... An interesting finding of Xerox Learning Systems' recent practices is the marketing executive's views about what those needs are. For example, 63% of sales vice presidents, 61% of national managers, and 60% of marketing vice presidents said they would definitely select or consider selecting product knowledge as a training topic. Yet only 36% of sales training managers said they would do so. With results of that type, it just may be that the first training need of most companies is to get management together to discuss training priorities.

Once the needs have been identified or known, the most puzzling questions faced by many senior managers in today's scenario are: Should I use external expertise? Why? What can I expect the outsider to bring to the situation?

External faculty/trainers have much to offer and can ensure your project many of the following advantages:

- Breadth of experience in the situation and/or the subject area and/or the type of organisation involved.
- Up-to-date skills and knowledge in relevant areas.
- An objective viewpoint.
- Willingness to question established norms or accepted practices.
- Specialised expertise.
- Credibility or value perceived as greater than that of internal staff (sometimes unfair but nonetheless true!).
- Freedom from worry about hierarchies and relative seniorities of staff and management.
- Willingness and ability to speak freely and listen to people and managers at all levels within the organisation.
- Trainees within the organisation will be more open and willing to listen and heed the outsider.
- They are not affected or constrained by internal politics.

As we have seen, training has a significant role to play. Whoever does the training (and the responsibility should be with the line management), it is important, being linked to change, improvement and, ultimately, to the enhanced well-being of the organisation. Yet, training can only have this role if it is successful in two ways: it must be **credible** and **effective**. Time needs to be spent on achieving this. But as the Bible puts it: "By their deeds ye shall know them." The ultimate assurance of credibility is to know your subject and provide good training – and that, in turn, means it must be effective.

I am reminded of the story about an oilman who once told a missionary (as they were being evacuated from Malaya ahead of a Japanese advance during World War II): "My life's work has gone into oil wells, which I had to blow up; your life has gone into people, into their character and development. My life's work has gone; yours will remain. I've failed and you have succeeded."

The best investment is an investment in people and their development. Remember: Money spent on the brain is never spent in vain!

ooo

24 Rules for Training Meetings

Here are 24 important dos and don'ts to remember during meetings:

1. **Break the ice at the start of a meeting.** Express your appreciation of this opportunity to discuss your topic. Explain that the use of the principles you are about to present to your unit will result in a reduction of their problems, reducing their work and worries. Indicate that this is an informal group and that you would welcome questions and comments.
2. **Know your subject "cold".** Be clear about the objectives and content for the session. Prepare a brief outline. Follow it.
3. **Be punctual.** Begin on time. *Close on time!*
4. **Radiate enthusiasm for your "cause".** Try to generate equal enthusiasm among members of your group. If you really believe that yours is a "cause", it will be "caught" by many people in the group.
5. **Outline what you propose to present.** Be clear about how much time you will devote to each topic. *Operate on a time schedule!*
6. **Avoid including too many things in the session.** It is better to put across a few important points thoroughly than to skim over a large number of concepts.
7. **Keep things handy.** Have your necessary accessories ready – notes, materials, demonstration items and so on.
8. **Go beyond mere learning.** When group members demonstrate that they have learned, it's not enough! Get them to do something about it! *Throughout your presentation, ensure real motivation!*
9. **Ensure respect for the leader.** Make sure the group displays a positive and respectful attitude towards you, their leader. Success in learning is often determined by the learner's attitude towards the instructor.
10. **Capitalise on everyone's knowledge.** Capitalise on the knowledge and intelligence that exist in the minds of group members. Their combined training and experience will supply many valuable ideas. Let the group (and yourself) benefit from group discussion.
11. **Be focussed.** *Don't let yourself or the discussion be sidetracked.* If an item scheduled for later discussion is brought up, simply say so

and resume the current point. Tactfully avoid irrelevant issues. There are many topics that would seem interesting to discuss! But if you are to complete your topic in the time allotted, *you must stick to the subject and the schedule.*

12. **Avoid a condescending tone.** Don't "talk down" to the group; you will insult their intelligence and antagonise them. Don't "highbrow" them by talking "over their heads". Use their language. Avoid unfamiliar words and expressions. Explain technical terms. Napoleon was said to have given three instructions to secretaries who relayed his messages: (1) Be clear! (2) Be clear! (3) Be clear!

13. **Don't give a speech.** Be as emphatic as necessary, especially in summarising, but don't orate. Appear to talk to each member of the group by moving your eyes frequently from one to another.

14. **Make your ideas palatable.** Use illustrative stories – humorous, if possible – that "clinch" a point.

15. **Speak clearly and distinctly.** Make sure you are heard by all present. Remember that your group has only one opportunity to hear what you have to say. If they don't get it the first time, they never will.

16. **Respect even the least intelligent group member.** *Never humiliate a person in the presence of others*. Find something good in his/her remarks. If not, tactfully avoid comment.

17. **Avoid eccentric personal habits.** Avoid twirling or repeatedly handling small articles; don't repeatedly adjust your tie, scratch your anatomy or stroke your chin. Don't smoke or chew gum while instructing!

18. **Evince real interest in others' viewpoints.** Show that you appreciate their contributions to the group discussion.

19. **Maintain patience and poise.** Remember that self-control is the first mark of the truly mature person. If you find yourself doing something wrong, don't betray yourself by excitement or self-criticism. Correct yourself – unobtrusively.

20. **Ask direct, specific questions of the group as a whole, expecting volunteered replies.** If no one answers, wait for a few seconds, then address one person by name and ask if he/she has a suggestion or idea to offer.

21. **Use the whiteboard in an organised manner.** Write and draw clearly enough for all to see. Stand apart so that the group can see your sketches or notes while you explain them – don't talk to the whiteboard!

22. **After each session stay around for a few minutes at the intermission.** Some group members may have matters they wish to discuss. Both you and the members will benefit from talks after the formal session has closed.

23. **After leaving the group, analyse your performance.** Ask yourself what you did wrong, what you can do better, what you forgot to do and so on. Only by self-analysis and self-criticism can you improve.

24. **Review your performance as an instructor.** Ask yourself the following questions: Did I achieve the lesson's objective? Did the lesson plan adequately cover the subject? Did the students master the lesson? Should any phase of the lesson be re-taught? Would other teaching methods have produced better results?

ooo

Winning Your Way in Selling!

Here, we present some winning tips for salespeople:

Control the ball: Let's think back to the very last time you lost a sale you wanted very much.

Who controlled the ball – you or the customer?

Who was on the offensive and who was on the defensive – you or your customer?

Before you began your presentation did you plan what you were going to do in the opening play?

Chances are the answers to all three questions will indicate that you let the customer control the ball, you were on the defensive and you neglected the very simple act of planning your opening play... what you were going to say and how you were going to say it.

Let's talk more about controlling the ball as a salesman. Controlling the ball in selling means things like knowing your product(s) intimately... and knowing your competitor's product(s) intimately, too. It also implies knowing the salesman you are competing with – his good points, his weak points and his manner of doing business.

Controlling the ball requires a firm understanding of your company and its policies so that you can answer a customer's questions promptly and with authority.

It is about knowing how to open a sale, how to make an effective sales presentation and how to close a sale. It means you know your product, your company and yourself so well that you are filled with confidence – so that when you are with a customer, you control the direction of negotiations. In short, controlling the ball means you know your job. You are a pro.

"When the going gets tough, you get tougher. And win!"

Make that second effort: The second effort is one of the keystones for success in selling. The second effort pays off. By being dedicated to making the second effort, many an ordinary salesman can become a star salesman.

You may have seen rugby stars make that second effort – and win. A halfback is running with the ball... gets hit by a tackle that would bring down an ordinary player... but he twists, turns, refuses to go down and finally wriggles free... and goes on to make the winning touchdown.

A second effort works the same way in selling. A salesman runs into a "no" and "can't do business now" or some other sales obstacle. While many a salesman would heed this dismissal and fold his tent, the man who loves the second effort makes one more try... attempts a new tack... persists gently but firmly to present his case... and to push for an order.

Successful salespeople never quit selling: Irene Buckley began selling insurance in the 1930s. She still does! She turned 95 recently. She was slowed down a little one January when she fell and broke a bone in her upper arm. She did go to the doctor's – and while she was there, sold him a $50,000 life insurance policy!

The number one real estate broker in the United States is a Rumanian emigrant named Nicholas Barsan. Every four days, he sells a house. One-third of his commissions come from repeat customers. He still knocks on doors asking homeowners if they are ready to sell.

There is no better way to dramatise the importance of refusing to give up than by the term "second effort". It means making one more try, one more run, doing one more thing to overcome the resistance that has arisen.

The salesman who practises the second effort will become an effective salesman.

Mental toughness counts: Carry on, no matter what the obstacles. Simply refuse to give up. When the going gets tough, simply get tougher. That's how you will win.

This is what mental toughness is all about – and it is a quality that every salesman must develop. Being a salesman is no easy job. You are going to get turndowns. You will get complaints about your company, its products or services, despite your knowledge that such complaints are ill founded or without justification. More, you're going to have dark periods when sales are hard to come by. It's then that you must be mentally tough – when you must summon up your resolve to conquer despite difficulties. Simply because you know deep within that you have the ability, that you represent a fine company with great products and that if you persist, you'll make the sale – and many, many more. Also, that you will win many new devoted customers.

Control your negative thoughts and recognise that the pendulum will swing favourably for you – and that by continued, positive efforts, your sales and your spirits will soar.

Fatigue makes cowards of us all: This is a strange subject to introduce into a sales topic, isn't it? Maybe it is all right for a professional football team – but for a sales team! Or is it?

After all, isn't it true that the physical well-being of a salesman is vital to his success? This being the case, shouldn't it be a subject that you emphasise and talk about right out in the open?

When you come right down to it, the demands on a salesman who must make a presentation to a top or tough customer, or to a purchasing committee, can be just as exhausting and nerve-wracking an experience as playing in a championship game. Obviously, a salesman shouldn't go into such a situation tired, exhausted or with a hangover. He simply can't do a top-drawer selling job in this case.

Any man knows from his school days that a good physical condition stimulates a healthier mental outlook. Being "in the pink" physically helps a man think and act better... and when it comes to salesmen, to sell better.

Finally, if you don't like your job, nothing can make it satisfying. Remember, whether you like it or not, things are always going to be tough. So learn to enjoy the rough and tumble and take the rough with the smooth. A Tarzan anecdote should put things in perspective...

Tarzan came home after work and asked Jane to make him a triple scotch. He polished it off and asked for another one.

Jane: "Tarzan, I am concerned about your drinking. Every afternoon you come home and have two or three drinks."

Tarzan: "I can't help it, Jane. It's a jungle out there!"

So it doesn't matter how difficult a job is – if we like it, it won't be a jungle! There are many formulas for winning... but none of them work unless we do!

ooo

Telemarketing: Power of the Phone

In 1980, a highly perceptive *Times* journalist wrote: **"The most powerful marketing tool ever invented lies unused on the desks..."** Over 20 years on and well over a century after its invention, the telephone is finally earning its marketing stripes.

There is no question that the telephone has taken the sales profession by storm. In the hands of an artful caller, it's a formidable tool for focusing a proposal. After all, only one person can talk at a time and if you're clever enough to make sure it's you, a sale won't be long in coming. What's more, this purely auditory medium catapults prospects off their turf into neutral territory. There's no desk to hide behind when you approach someone over the phone. And those who get really good at selling on the phone find some efficient ways to corner the elusive 'animal' who lurks in the shadows of every business-to-business transaction: the person with the authority to say 'yes'. It's often more productive to make a few preliminary phone calls rather than drop in on a company without knowing who wields the power.

Selling on the telephone is an art that has to be learned, practised and continuously developed in line with your business.

Advantages of Telephone Selling

The telephone can get action fast. Prospects will have immediate information about your product or service and what it can do for them. Ideas can be formulated quickly. Selling is speedier because there is no sitting back, enjoying tea or coffee with the prospect. You have to get to the point without delay. The most effective means of getting ideas to the largest number of prospects in the shortest possible time is by telephone.

Personal selling day-by-day, driving, walking, waiting, more waiting, chatting and then face-to-face selling has one great drawback – inertia. It is difficult to get started. You sit making plans, thinking how good it is going to be and, by the time you are ready to start, it is time for lunch. The phone helps eliminate inertia – you simply pick up the receiver, dial (or press buttons) and talk. You will be so busy getting new numbers and telling your story, you will not have time to get discouraged. The telephone keeps you busy – and productive!

Whenever you attempt to sell by telephone you are simultaneously faced with an advantage and a disadvantage. Once you are through to your client you can talk directly, without interference, because the telephone takes precedence over everything and everyone else in the room. If you have never met before, you are as big (or small!) as the personality you project through your voice.

The following tips should improve your chances of success via the phone:

Roll out the role-playing: The difference between training provided for field salespeople and that given to telephone sales representatives (TSRs) is often amazing. Because TSRs must rely entirely on verbal skills to sell, they should be trained as thoroughly as field salespeople and role-playing is a critical component of that training. Prior to the training session, write out role-playing examples. Each should contain typical customer dialogue, including questions and objections. Have both the trainer and other TSRs review each role-play effort and provide feedback on the results of each contact.

Clumsy as it may seem at first, role-playing will improve as TSRs get more comfortable with it. It's a small price to pay for the self-confidence and professionalism that the new TSRs will feel when they have a real customer on the line.

At all costs, avoid overloading your TSRs. Telephone selling is a tough job and it is unrealistic to expect TSRs to complete 70 to 100 contacts per day without sounding like robots – and eventually burning out.

Be prepared: Before making an outbound call, prepare and practise a 25-to-40-second script that does the following:

- Clearly identifies who you are.
- Explicitly identifies your company.
- States the telephone number where you can be reached.
- Succinctly identifies the product or service you are selling.
- Explains why the customer should care about your call.
- Outlines WIIFM (What's in it for me?) or benefits to the person called.

Also do your homework and learn as much as possible about the people you're calling. Know:

- The name of your customers.
- Their area of interest.
- Their previous buying activity.

Use more open-ended questions: Many reps can't see the woods for the trees, so tell them to resist selling at the first opportunity. It's important to get the customer's full story before proposing anything and the secret to this is asking more comprehensive questions. Reverse the ratio and you're on the way to turning sales reps into account managers. Ideally, it should be about two-to-one in favour of open-ended questions.

"On a scale of eleven, how confident are you that this sale will actually happen?" Getting the customer to put a number on the likelihood of a sale can open all sorts of possibilities. (Make the scale at least 11. If you say 10, people tend to answer five.) If your contact comes back with seven, eight, or nine, you can say, "Terrific! What are some of the things we need to do to raise it to ten or eleven?"

If the customer responds with a three or four, it's time to do more research on the company!

Text. Tone. Timing: A major way telemarketing breaks down is when people sound canned, not fresh. Theoretically, scripts should work, but they often wind up in a drawer. Give reps the opportunity to improvise – then monitor the result.

Study phone calls that succeed, then abstract that into a "call path". Your tone of voice can make a world of difference in the outcome of a call, too.

Follow-up: In business-to-business selling, it often takes **five to seven interactions** before a prospect can be expected to seriously consider even a low-risk speculative change or new application. Your goal should be to use tele-contact for as many of those interactions as practical. In so doing, we preserve the precious face-to-face contact time of the field force for on-site demonstration and close.

So why is it that this most vital marketing tool has not gained the requisite importance? The reason why people fear making appointments or selling on the telephone is because no one likes being rejected. It is important to understand that this feeling of rejection is perfectly normal. It won't go away, so don't waste time worrying about it. The prospect may be out, tied up on another call, in a meeting or can't be disturbed. Even if you do make contact there is no guarantee that you are going to get a 'Yes'. In fact, it is more than likely you will get a 'No'.

Telephoning for appointments or to make a sale is a numbers game. The more calls you make, the more appointments/sales you will complete – it's called the law of averages! You are not going to sell to everyone you phone, but the number you sell to will be in proportion to the number you call. Initially, it may be two per cent. If you phone 200 people, you will sell to four people. If you phone 500, you will sell to 10 people. Once this principle is accepted, you are well on your way to success. As you do more telephone selling, you will improve; your technique will gradually become more skilful because, as with any other activity, practise tends to make you perfect.

You will be told that luck plays a great part in this when you are really successful in selling by phone. A regular comment will be: "You're lucky!" Remember, then, that the real meaning of 'luck' is when thorough preparation meets an opportunity.

Let your fingers do the walking – but the talking and selling is up to you!

○○○

How and When to Conduct Sales Meetings

Being engaged in sales, one tends to hold more meetings, conferences, lectures and general get-togethers than almost any other field. For this reason, one must do several things to ensure the necessity, purpose and success of the meetings. Consequently, knowledge of how to hold a successful group meeting is important to each group leader, whether he is the training director of a hundred salespersons or a unit manager of just four salespersons.

Lost Sales Time

Group meetings take time and effort on the part of the meeting leader and others who participate. Considerable additional costs could be incurred for accommodation, facilities and visual aids. Most important of all, perhaps, is the time that salespeople lose by attending meetings during their working day. If the meeting is successful, these costs are justified, for good sales training pays off in increased sales. However, too many meetings don't accomplish anything. As someone once said, "I always come to meetings with a problem. I always leave with a briefing and a problem!"

But successful meetings don't just happen. They require careful consideration of our basic requirements for meeting success:

1. The meeting must be carefully planned.

2. The physical aids and the speakers must be prepared.
3. The meeting must be properly conducted.
4. The material to be covered must be presented in a way that the objectives of the meeting are achieved.

Planning the Meeting

It is impossible to say which of the steps is the most important, since all are essential. But it is safe to say that planning for meetings is the most often neglected. Four-hour meetings have been held for which the total planning time was 15 minutes. The results could have been expected – disorganised sessions that did not accomplish their objectives.

Adequate planning requires answers to a series of questions:
1. Why is the meeting being held? (Is it necessary?)
2. Who is to make the presentation?
3. What subject matter should be included?
4. How is the material to be presented?
5. When is each presentation to be made?

Why hold the meeting? This first question seems so obvious that it hardly deserves an answer. Yet many unit meetings are a waste of time and money simply because this obvious question was not answered. "To train" is not an adequate answer, nor is: "We always hold meetings on Monday mornings." Too many training meetings are held because it seems the thing to do or the boss says meetings should be held. When this is the case, the salespeople often get nothing of value from it – except a coffee and a joke they can use maybe – because the meeting leader himself has no clear idea of what is to be accomplished.

Have specific meeting objectives: No sales meeting should be started until the leader has clearly thought through the specific reasons for holding it. The specific meeting objectives should always be written out and followed. The objectives of a meeting should be limited.

As a group leader sits down to list the objectives, he/she can encounter another problem: How to cover many things in a single meeting. So, he/she must decide on the objectives to be covered. No general rule applies, but remember that a sales representative can comprehend and get more from a one-hour meeting that covers two or three objectives than he can in a four-hour meeting with 15 to 20 objectives. In the latter case, they may not get anything from the meeting but end up being hopelessly confused!

When the above is considered, a leader will probably find he has more objectives written down than can be covered effectively. Which should he eliminate? A careful inspection may reveal that many objectives are not basic ones and would not apply to the situation at this time. From the list remaining, he/she should choose those that are most important and can be adequately covered in the time period established.

It is perfectly okay to advise attendees in advance of the purpose and objectives of your meetings, but it is unwise to establish an agenda indicating the time that each subject will be covered. By indicating a specific time on the agenda, you can endanger certain subjects by either moving to them before the previous topic is resolved or carrying a topic beyond its conclusion. Also, some attendees might be more interested in the 10:15 coffee break than they are in the meeting's content.

It is far more effective to schedule additional meetings if you want to cover more than three or four objectives.

Who is to make the presentation? Often, a leader can best utilise the talents of members of his group or unit. It doesn't follow that the leader must always "have the floor". Perhaps there is an attendee in your meeting who is well versed in one of your objectives. He can be invaluable, as most or all of the attendees are aware of his knowledge in that field. Besides, the more genuine participation you have in a meeting, the more interest will be developed.

The person therefore must:

(a) Have knowledge of the subject matter.

(b) Have the ability as a speaker or teacher.

A group will listen with more attention to two speakers talking for 30 minutes each, than one making a 60-minute presentation. Wherever possible, a unit manager or group leader should include another unit manager, or even a member of his/her unit, to share speaking responsibilities.

What subject matter should be included? The planner should prepare an outline, as there is always the danger of giving the sales representatives too much information, as well as the danger of too little information. It is far more effective to schedule additional meetings if you want to cover more than three or four objectives.

Showmanship

Lastly, meetings may sometimes need showmanship too. In his book, *Handbook for Successful Sales Meetings*, Bill N. Newman told of the time a sales promotion manager devised a sensational way to introduce a new merchandising aid. He conducted a coroner's inquest! A few days before the meeting, he showed the new aid to several top salesmen. In the interest of field-testing, a few were permitted to use it. Then came the meeting.

When the sales promotion manager was introduced, there was no mention of his subject. As he rose to speak, a recording of a funeral march was played. A mock funeral procession entered from the rear of the room, led by an "undertaker", complete with dark suit and stovepipe hat! Two "pallbearers" followed, carrying a "casket". When the procession reached the front of the room, the speaker called it to a halt. The music was also stopped and the emcee asked for an explanation. The "undertaker" explained: "We're burying an unsuccessful salesman."

When asked the cause of death, the "undertaker" replied: "I don't know but we're burying all of them. Something is putting an end to all unsuccessful salesmen."

The speaker had the casket placed on a table while a coroner's inquest was conducted. Ten "witnesses" were called to the front and seated apart from the audience. They were questioned one at a time. The first expressed the opinion that unsuccessful salesmen were being eliminated by a new sales aid. Other witness confirmed the opinion. Salesmen who had field-tested the item told of their success in using it. By carefully selecting the "witnesses" and asking well-prepared questions, the speaker had painted a very rosy picture.

A gavel was banged and the verdict announced: "The findings are that death was caused by the new sales aid. This new aid is putting an end to all unsuccessful sales efforts."

At that moment, the "corpse" jumped out of the "casket"!

It was a real shocker since the audience had no reason to believe someone was actually in the box! He ran to the speaker's stand and grabbed the new sales aid. Then he raced out of the room yelling, "Don't bury me – I want to use it, too!"

This event lasted only 22 minutes. But it did ten times as much good as a speech of the same duration. Try it!

ooo

Managing Bad Debt: The Importance of Good Cash Collection Skills

A bird in hand is better than a lakh rupees in the bush. The bird at least guarantees that evening's dinner. But a debtor beating around the bush with lakhs of rupees can often turn out to be a bad dream.

Volatile business conditions of recent years have created problems of cash flow and interest charges that were never before encountered. Companies large and small have (in many cases for the first time) come to realise that trade debtors or receivables on the balance sheet represent a very substantial and expensive component of capital employed. They are also now beginning to accept that trade debtors represent an investment in the marketplace on which the expected return is the profit to be earned only when payment has completed the sale. At the same time, like all investments, those trade debtors are subject to the risks arising from the effect of the economic climate on that marketplace generally.

The most precious risk to a company's profit on the sale is, however, by way of interest expense from non-payment to time. In essence, that is what credit management is all about and its objective can be said to be "to have the highest possible debtors (sales) for the shortest possible time (collection/profit)".

Has it ever occurred to you that before the customer buys your goods, both are interested (he in your goods and you in his money), but once he gets the goods, he is not interested – it's only you who are (for your money!).

Research consistently shows that, on an average, a typical invoice will be settled in not less than 72 to 78 days. As 30-day terms are normal, the extra 48 days have a significant effect on profit and loss. It can even be the critical factor affecting a company's survival.

Therefore, a good cash collection procedure can make the difference between a profitable business and one forced into liquidation because of slow payments and default on outstanding debts. An unpaid debt is a loan being financed by your company. It means many companies are prevented from achieving their full potential because, instead of using borrowed money to develop and grow their business, they have to borrow money just to fund their own sales ledgers.

One question I am asked constantly by salespeople is: "Is it the salesperson's job to collect cheques?" In answering this, I run the risk of alienating myself from many members of my profession because I have always been of the opinion that the number one cause of bad debts – "write-offs" – and corporate cash flow problems is the salesperson's lack of skill in this vital element of the sale. Why this lack of skill?

Here are some of the most common reasons:

- Many salespeople ignore the fact that a "sale" is only a "sale" when the goods or services are paid for!
- A number of salespeople consider "asking for a cheque" to be a menial task, which should be carried out by clerks in the accounts department.
- Others see their job as: "My role is to get the order, not to waste time collecting cheques!"
- Few sales induction programmes offer advice or are held in getting payments, with the result that money is rarely mentioned at the sales call presentation.
- Some salespeople, understandably too, have enough difficulty getting the order without putting it at risk by haggling over payment terms!
- Too many salespeople think only in terms of getting the best deal for the customer and forget that they are obliged to get the best terms for their company as well.

You may be thinking this does not apply to your organisation and if that is the case you are fortunate indeed. However, several companies do have such problems and the only differing factor is the name of the company. If this problem exists within your own organisation, recognise the futility of changing the system; as the root cause of the problem is elsewhere – in the attitudes and the improper training of personnel in collection procedures and techniques. Until such time that you can bring about a change via proper training, your cash flow difficulties will continue to escalate.

Remember that cash is to business what blood is to the body – allow it to drain away and the body becomes weak and eventually dies.

ooo

Caring for Your Customer – Part 1

The Importance of Good Customer Care

It may take 15 years to build a relationship with a customer but it can take only 15 seconds to destroy it! Research reveals that it costs five times (or more) to win a new customer than to keep an existing one. Any company whose future depends on "getting the business and keeping it" should recognise that everybody who has an interface with customers must have the skills to deal promptly, efficiently and courteously with anybody who phones, calls or writes.

Why is it so important to treat every customer like a millionaire? One reason is that you never know which customers might really be millionaires! John Barrier taught managers at US Bank of Washington a lesson in customer service they'll never forget. It all began when he went to encash a $25 cheque. In his Acme Concrete Co. baseball cap and dungarees, Barrier looked like an ordinary customer.

Afterwards, he tried to drive his pickup truck out of the parking lot. But the kid at the counter told Barrier to cough up 60 cents or else go back inside and get his parking ticket stamped to verify that he was a bank customer.

Annoyed, Barrier re-parked his pickup, went back into the bank and presented his ticket to a teller – who refused to validate it. Perhaps she didn't believe Barrier had really made a transaction at the bank. Maybe she thought he'd just walked in off the street.

"I'm about to make another transaction in your bank," Barrier said. "Give me the $1 million I keep here. I'm taking it next door."

US Bank decided to validate his parking ticket after all, but it was too late. The multimillionaire real estate developer got a new bank – and US Bank was out $1,000,000.60!

All too often we neither give good service nor get it. Instead, we whine. We pass the buck. Our whining anthem is, "It's not my department!"

Jan Carlson, the president of Scandinavian airlines, in his book *Moments of Truth*, claimed that in one year his staff came in contact with 10 million customers approximately five times. The contact lasted on average 15 seconds each time. He goes on to say: "Thus SAS is created in the minds of the customers 50 million times a year, 15 seconds at a time. They are the moments when we must prove to our customers that SAS is the best alternative."

To be successful in the marketplace it is important to be 'positively different'. According to the experts (and by that I mean the buyers), if a company demonstrates it can provide top-quality service consistently, it will be successful in any market conditions.

The biggest single influence on retaining customers is their perception of how much you 'care'. We all want new customer business but how many of us go out of our way to look after them? We can all quote numerous examples of where we were treated unprofessionally. Generally, when I ask people to give examples of when they received 'consistent outstanding service' from any organisation, they take time to reply. You phone a bank wanting to know your bank balance – you are snapped back at with: "Sorry, we cannot update your balance now as we are extremely busy – come tomorrow in person and check."

Dun and Bradstreet carried out a survey that revealed some interesting information, i.e., 16% of buyers stop buying every year for the following reasons:

- 1% die
- 3% change jobs or move away
- 5% favour friends
- 9% change for better prices
- 82% are unhappy with suppliers.

There may be little we can do to save the first 18% but the other 82% is very much within the control and capability of most organisations. By doing so you not only help increase profits but are also securing your own position.

If that last major lot of dissatisfied customers have not bothered to complain and are asked the reason, these are some of their most frequent responses, which invariably never reach the supplier of the service:

- I don't think my complaint is welcomed.
- I don't suppose anyone will listen to me.
- I have tried complaining, but nothing has happened.
- Whenever I make a complaint, I am treated with suspicion.
- Complaining is more trouble than finding a new source.

When service becomes the topic of conversation, dissatisfaction is usually a more popular topic than satisfaction. According to a survey published in *Harpers* magazine, USA, if you are satisfied with a service, your satisfaction will only be communicated to your own inner circle of eight people on an average, but if you are dissatisfied, your dissatisfaction will be communicated to anyone you get a chance to do so – 22 people on an average! With dissatisfaction being such a popular subject, in all probability these 22 listeners will in turn pass on this new information to their own clique or circle (average eight people), thus causing one dissatisfied customer spreading this information to approximately 176 people (22 × 8 = 176)!

Consultant Walter Geier once asked a successful businessman the secret of his success. The man replied: "I take all the customers nobody else wants. I go out of my way to get the complainers, the tough customers and the ones who are never satisfied... They appreciate good service when they get it. And they know how rare it is. So they stay with you... Also, their friends know how hard they are to please. So they tend to follow them... But most of all, tough customers keep me and my employees on our toes, they won't let us get careless or overconfident for a moment."

In today's competitive market, customers have a choice. If we cannot give them what they are looking for, they can always get it somewhere else.

Creating a culture of service in your company requires discipline. What should you do if you overhear an employee telling a customer any version of "It's not my department"? First, save the customer, fast. Rush over to the customer and say, "It is my department. What can I do to make you happy?" Have the employee who said, "It's not my department," stay right with you while, together, you make the customer happy.

Next, make an example of the incident – not the employee – to impress the point on everyone else. Call a meeting and say: "I just heard someone say, 'It's not my department' to a customer." Then show them the right way to do it.

○○○

Caring for Your Customer – Part II

Most faults can be corrected by professional training in the relevant skills. There is a little difference between the people who project a rather poor company image and those who project the opposite. The little difference is *attitude*; the big difference is whether the attitude is positive or negative.

Many poor customer service problems stem from the staff being allowed to develop bad habits. Through encouragement, coaching and monitoring, if you can bring about a change in attitude, the habits will change automatically.

Here are some suggestions to carry out an effective customer care programme: 'Welcoming people into your company', 'Handling complaints' and 'Customer service practice'.

Welcoming People into Your Company

1. Look the person in the eye.
2. Smile warmly.
3. Greet the person with a friendly 'Good morning/afternoon'.
4. Say 'How can I help you?' Avoid 'Can I help you?' It sometimes conveys: 'What the hell are you doing here?'
5. Question skilfully and wait until the person explains the purpose of the call. Not everybody is capable of explaining precisely what they are looking for and they may need help.
6. Briefly summarise the visitor's request to ensure you have got the message correctly. Get the caller's name and use it.
7. Avoid saying, 'He is not available', or 'We do not sell them anymore' without offering a realistic alternative.
8. Explain what you are going to do and how long it will take, if appropriate.
9. If possible, offer the visitor coffee or a newspaper. This keeps him or her away from the counter or reception area and allows others to get on with their work.
10. Do not leave the visitor in the dark. If the request is taking longer than anticipated, explain this and keep him or her informed of the progress.

11. When your business is completed, give your name so that the visitor can get back to a 'person', not a 'department', if he/she has any further queries.
12. Few people do it, but it makes such a difference saying, 'Thank you for the business, Mr/Mrs.... Please come back and see us again'. It does wonders for the parting impression.

Handling Customer Problems

1. Listen. Listen. Listen (show concern). A most important skill in handling conflict is the ability to pay attention with all your senses. Avoid trying to calm the other person down; this will only make the situation worse.

2. Ask appropriate questions to elicit facts. The only way you can demonstrate your 'real interest' in the other's point of view is by asking questions. Take notes as you go along for the purpose of summarising when appropriate. Ask open-ended questions such as why, what, when etc.

3. Summarise the points at issue. Demonstrate your understanding of the issues by summarising with, 'If I understand you correctly, this is the situation...' Ensure the customer agrees with your interpretation.

4. Find an area of agreement and state it. It will be a rare case where a customer will have it so wrong that there are no areas of agreement. Even conceding a small point may add to a conciliatory atmosphere – something like, 'Mr/Mrs...., I agree with you; if we said we would deliver on Tuesday and you did not receive it until Thursday, that is totally unacceptable and I would be just as angry.' Alternatively, if you or your company are at fault for the entire complaint, apologise, get it out of the way and take appropriate action. Customers accept things do go wrong now and then; the critical point is how the complaint is handled.

5. Demonstrate empathy. Customers do not always expect you to agree with them but what all of them can justifiably expect is that you will do your utmost to understand their point of view. Empathy allows us to demonstrate without having to agree. Bearing in mind that the complaint may be based on a lack of information on the customer's part, saying he or she is wrong or that you don't agree is not likely to help an already difficult situation. Empathy is expressed thus: 'I can understand how you feel about it, Mr/Mrs.... and if I were in that situation I am sure I would be just as annoyed. However, there is another viewpoint that I would request you to consider...' There should never be a situation where

an employee has to use 'I disagree with you' or 'We will have to agree to differ'. By mentioning 'disagreement' you are highlighting the fact that you are in conflict.

6. Agree on the action or follow-up. Whatever agreement is made between you and the customer should be followed up with full speed. Complaints are an inevitable part of business but how they are handled will dictate your company's future relationship with the customer.

7. Thank the customer for the complaint! The customer has a choice: to bring the complaint directly to you or take it to your competitor. Those who bring their complaints directly to you should be thanked. Sometimes a brief note to the customer, thanking him or her for taking the time to contact you and giving you the opportunity to correct it, will do a lot for the business relationship. Many people protest by taking their business elsewhere. You could prevent this by thanking them for bringing the complaint to your notice.

8. Share this information internally, so that others in the organisation learn of the situation and make improvements.

Finally, to help you remember the importance of good customer care, remember the CARE principle (Customers Are Really Everything), which is summed up in the acronym.

You also need to ensure the following:

- **Promptness:** Be prepared and willing to immediately be of service. The 'Yes, I can!' attitude and promptness in acting inspire confidence.
- **Reliability:** Customers should be able to trust you and repose complete confidence in your services.
- **Accuracy:** Cultivate the ability to observe and act with precision.
- **Courtesy:** Be gracious, obliging and polite.
- **Tactfulness:** Learn to say the right thing without offence.
- **Information:** Communicate the relevant information and the current progress when handling queries or any new circumstances that will affect him or her.
- **Competence:** The ability and capacity to carry out a task. Don't pass the blame on to someone else.
- **Empathy:** Identification with the other person and his or her problem. Listen carefully without interruption, putting yourself in the customer's shoes.

ooo

32 Ways to Motivate Your Sales Team – And Yourself!

Big bonuses, high commissions and irresistible incentives alone will not get maximum results from salespeople. Although you must provide incentives, you should also face this truth: Almost all of us must motivate **ourselves** to act in our **own** best interest. To stay motivated, find the best way to motivate yourself.

Warren Lester was asked why he was such a successful salesperson. He replied: "I tell myself every night when I go bed that I lost my job and tomorrow I must start from scratch." Lester further explained that the reason he did this was because a man in a strange job always gives it his best.

The toughest part of any job is getting started on it – because achieving the things that do us the most good is seldom easy. If you think your salespeople have trouble getting started, don't think it's a problem peculiar to them. About 99% of all the people you know have the same problem – just as you do yourself. It takes a lot more power to get a car started than it does to keep it rolling.

Here are a series of powerful self-starters for you – and your people:

1. **Put your plans into writing:** Spell out in your mind, and preferably on paper, exactly what must be done, and how, to accomplish the goal.

2. **Be more specific with yourself:** How specific are you with yourself in analysing problems and working out plans? Are these plans made in terms of what you are going to say, to whom you will say it, under what circumstances and when?

3. **Assign yourself a small part of the job:** Faced with a major activity, break it down into fractions. Assign yourself 10%, 5% or even 2% of the total; the important thing is to start on a small portion so that you don't say, "I don't have the time."

4. **Use a self-motivating system:** It is not enough to make a plan and then check when it should have been completed. You need a series of checkpoints. For example, if you intend to see ten people by the weekend, you might check yourself on Tuesday and Thursday.

5. **Use self-prompting:** You must keep prompting and nudging yourself on the expected results. People always do something because they expect to get some benefit. By repeatedly calling the benefit to our own attention, we motivate ourselves.

6. **Avoid self-temptation:** If you wish to motivate yourself to do something, you should deliberately and consciously avoid circumstances that motivate you *not* to do it, to put it off or to forget about it.

7. **Set an early start:** If you have something to do which you have been putting off, get to the office a couple of hours early and dig into it. This has several advantages. For example, an early start shows a determination to get something out of the way. Also, most people work better in the early morning hours.

8. **Stop expecting to be superhuman:** You achieve more by analysing your limitations and taking them into account than by refusing to recognise them.

9. **Take advantage of differences in self-motivation ability:** Many people operate according to a habitual schedule, which does not take into account the tremendous variation in their psychological ability at various times during the day. Take advantage of high inspiration peaks.

10. **Sell yourself on taking chances:** Starting to do the wrong thing is preferable to doing nothing. Once you can see you are off course you can alter it, but at least you have started something. Why not cultivate the habit of "living experimentally"? Give new methods a try.

11. **Use negative self-motivation:** You can prove yourself with a reminder of the unfavourable consequences that will arise if you do not take action. This type of motivation is especially useful when procrastination comes from indifference.

12. **Improve your priority schedule:** Have you ever compared the priority you should give that you actually do give to each part of your work? Keep a time control budget and analyse your records.

13. **Be definite with yourself about when:** Tell yourself the specific day and hour you intend to do something and be sure to act at the scheduled time.

14. **Distinguish between "can't" and "don't want to":** When people explain that they can't do something, they often mean that they really don't want to do it. Isn't this a habit we all have?

15. **Find additional ways to feel more adequate:** Self-confidence is a feeling that you are able to do whatever you must. Anything improving your knowledge or skill increases your self-confidence. Right now, why not jot down a list of ways to increase your job knowledge and skills?

16. **Get started:** People associate confidence with action and a lack of action with a lack of confidence. You can use this principle by forcefully taking action.

17. **Improve your self-persuasion skills:** Whether or not you apply what you know depends largely on your self-persuasion skills. This is true of actions that aren't particularly exciting or pleasant. To motivate yourself to take action you will find it helpful to ask yourself some questions:

    (a) What am I putting off that I should finish?
    (b) Why am I putting this off? What is causing my reluctance?
    (c) When is the best time to do this? Why not now?
    (d) Am I assuming that it will be better to do this later?
    (e) What are the disadvantages of putting it off?

18. **Predict success to overcome inertia:** Predict that you will be successful in doing something or that the chance of success is reasonable. A positive mental attitude enables you to sufficiently increase your self-motivation to overcome obstacles.

19. **Decide what needs to be done first:** Several types of movements or procedure are connected with any activity. If we don't decide exactly what operations need to be carried out, we tend to do nothing.

20. **Invest daily in a positive mental attitude:** Most of us give lip service to the value of self-confidence but fail to generate and maintain a feeling for it. All of us constantly encounter minor disappointments and we need something to offset them. Try to associate with successful people. Read books that make you feel more confident and informed.

21. **Read literature dealing directly with your problem:** Most of us underestimate the knowledge found in books and magazines of good quality. Your self-motivational ability depends on finding a method you can be enthusiastic about. The more methods you are familiar with – reading, listening, observing, experimenting – the greater your chances of finding one that fits you.

22. **Contradict negative thoughts:** If you have doubts about ability, short-circuit them by asking yourself: What makes me think I can't do it?

23. **Use self-signalling devices:** Do you forget things overnight? Here's a sure-fire cure: Write yourself a note, leave it just where you eat breakfast and put something on top of it that must be moved before you can put down your plate. Another method: Tape a note to the bathroom mirror that will stare at you while you use the mirror.

24. **Promise yourself an immediate reward for doing something:** This technique ensures you motivate yourself to do the necessary work.

25. **Do extra work just after you get good news:** This is one of the best times to do extra work. You feel optimistic, and optimism makes difficult jobs seem easy. Don't waste this time or mood in routine activities, but dig into the difficult ones.

26. **Avoid negative suggestions from others:** Anyone who has tried some method and failed to use it successfully is often too eager to tell you how it didn't work for him. Never accept this as the final assessment of methods for you.

27. **Recognise conflict and make a definite choice:** As long as there's conflict about what to do, most people's tendency is to do nothing. Make a clear-cut decision. It may not be easy, but it is essential.

28. **Give yourself the right to make mistakes:** Some people's motivational difficulties may stem from the idea that they must

do something perfectly or not at all. Since there are few things any of us do perfectly, this attitude places great limitations on us.

29. **Exercise your sense of humour:** By investing in your sense of humour you make a definite investment in a positive mental attitude. Whatever makes you laugh helps give you a more realistic viewpoint. It should be practised and given high priority.

30. **Use action language:** Use words such as "now", "immediately", "at once". They influence us into prompt action; they help us get started and to overcome tendencies towards procrastination.

31. **Expect more and you will get more:** In a study of schoolteachers it turned out that when they held high expectations from their students this alone was enough to ensure an increase of 25 points in the students' IQ scores.

32. **Find that "hot button":** JP Morgan once proved that you can motivate anybody if you find their "hot button". His sister could never get her son (who was away at college) to answer her letters. Morgan wrote a letter and said: "Enclosed is a ten-dollar note" and he deliberately didn't enclose the money! He immediately received a reply saying, "The ten dollars you said was enclosed in your letter wasn't."

○○○

Ongoing Coaching for Sales Personnel

One of the most important responsibilities of any sales manager is the training and development of each sales representative in order to increase their productivity. Nothing will improve a sales representative's performance more than regular on-the-job coaching.

In this context, coaching may be defined as the process of providing each individual with the information, skills, work habits and attitudes required to maintain effective territory coverage and to equal or exceed the performance standards of top-level producers in every required activity.

Profitable sales volume does not result from just making information available either by the written or spoken word. There is a wide difference between having the information "in your head" and using it skilfully to build sales volumes.

It helps getting less experienced salespeople into profitable production faster; it helps the experienced salesperson increase sales volume and build a strong sales organisation.

Before a manager can attain top-flight performance as a sales coach, pass on valuable know-how and develop each salesperson's full potential, it is necessary for the manager to be able to:

1. Analyse a sale, step-by-step, to determine:
   (a) Those things that contributed to the success of the sale:
   (b) Those things that either held up the sale, slowed it down or caused failure.
2. Point out specific things that were well done, so that the salesperson can use and reuse them in future sales. Also, those methods, techniques or sales statements that should be strengthened or changed to add selling power to the salesperson's presentations.

Coaching would basically fall into four areas:

A. **Attitudes/behaviour:** The representative's outlook and the way he/she approaches the contact.

B. **Knowledge:** How well the representative knows the fundamentals of his/her job and product.

C. **Working skills:** How well he can apply what he/she knows and his/her techniques in so doing.

D. **General:** Any item not covered in the other three categories, such as appearance, use of time, self-evaluation etc.

In playing the role of a coach, what any front-line manager would need to really work upon is "the skills issue" or the "coaching" aspects on the job that need to be built in and covered. This follows a process of:

1. Understanding
2. Accepting
3. Remembering
4. Using

The various steps that need to be adopted in preparing a manager to undertake this "coaching" would be as follows:

1. Preparation of the manager to undertake this exercise himself.
2. Arrangements for the coaching and schedule.
3. Actual on-the-job coaching (observing calls and discussing).
4. Action plan (coaching calendar).
5. Development plans.
6. Documentation.

7. Follow-up (coaching calendar) till the determined degree of improvement.

Some of the characteristics a manager would want to observe regarding Attitudes:

1. Enthusiasm
2. Pride in company and product
3. Friendliness
4. Aggressiveness
5. Self-confidence

Some of the issues a manager would want to observe concerning Knowledge:

1. Product knowledge, technicalities and industry knowledge
2. Rates
3. Company policy
4. Customer needs
5. Business functions in general and of specific customer involved in coaching contact
6. Market conditions

Some guidelines a manager would want to observe concerning Working Skills:

1. Use of a planned approach
2. Personal manner
3. Use of clues from premises
4. Phrasing and asking of key questions
5. Recognising and following up clues
6. Handling the customer as an individual personality
7. Listening and observation
8. Recording information
9. Use of a pre-call guide
10. Exploring customer needs thoroughly
11. Evaluating and organising recommendations
12. Use of sales aids and testimonial
13. Communication skills: concise, precise and in simple language

Preparation

What should be considered in evaluating preparation?

   i. Understanding current level
      - Previous Coaching Reports will provide areas of past weaknesses and strength.
   ii. Observing current selling skill levels
      - In office – Preparation
      - In field – Sales skill
   iii. Study of performance of calls/closures
      - No. of calls (fresh/follow-up)
      - No. of presentations
      - No. of closes
      - Others
   iv. Study time spent in office
      - In field
   v. Reporting status/cheque bounce/history
   vi. Pending accounts yet to be closed.

Approach

What should be considered in evaluating the approach?

1. Professional introduction
2. Gaining customer interest
3. Speaking clearly, confidently, pleasantly
4. Making a good initial impression on the customer
5. Arousing curiosity
6. Enhancing the client's self-image.

Probing

What should be considered in evaluating probing?

1. Effective use of open and closed probing covering Current Desires & Barriers of each of the following: Product, Market, Competitors, etc.
2. Did the probes reveal business needs and wants? Were they acknowledged?
3. Relevancy of probes (i.e., "Mr/Ms Client, what do you consider to be your major business problem?") will prove more effective than "How's business?"

Presentation
What should be considered when evaluating the presentation?
1. Selling value (as an answer to a businessperson's needs)
2. Use of sales aids
3. Reasons for buying
4. Control of presentation
5. Speaking the customer's language
6. Creating desire.

Recommendation
What should be considered when evaluating the recommendation?
1. Positive quality of recommendation (Did the representative recommend his programme convincingly?)
2. Presentation of recommendation in terms of customer's needs and support with use of benefits: Plan A or Plan B?
3. Completeness of recommendation (Did representative's recommendation cover pertinent marketing areas, etc.)
4. Clarity of recommendation (Was representative's recommendation programme clear to the customer?)
5. Ability to use "trial" closes (Does he/she employ closing techniques for customer reaction?)
6. Asking for sale (Does he/she convincingly strive for customer approval?)
7. Positive quality of close (Does he/she avoid a close that implies doubt?)
8. Did the customer take action?

Additional Factors
What additional factors should be considered?
1. Service attitude (Did representative leave customer with favourable impression?)
2. Accuracy (Did customer have a clear understanding of what he bought, etc.?)
3. Personal characteristics (appearance/voice, poise, enthusiasm, conduct, creative ability, etc.?)
4. If telephone sales, did representative instruct the customer that a signature was required or not required?
5. Future business considerations.

Coaching Discussion
Coaching discussions may be introduced in various ways:
1. Seek representative's own appraisal of his/her performance which:
   - ✓ Makes the instructions appear as a joint discussion rather than giving a teacher-student impression.
   - ✓ Encourages the habit of self-evaluation.
2. Recall some positive occurrence in the contact. When presentations are *good*, mention the outstanding points specifically and then comment on the less-than-satisfactory points. When the presentations are *not good*, emphasise the major weaknesses and demonstrate how they can be corrected.

What are the advantages of discussing the observed call step-by-step?
1. Gives an organised framework for discussion.
2. The manager can be sure he/she has covered all points.
3. Reminds the representative about steps of the contact.
4. Representative has more thorough evaluation of his/her workmanship.
5. Representative develops a better understanding of the standards for each step.

What are the advantages of discussing only the major areas requiring improvement?
1. Will not give the impression of nitpicking, since unimportant details are not covered.
2. Greater emphasis will be placed upon one or two major weaknesses.
3. Representative will not feel discouraged or frustrated having been shown too many weaknesses.
4. Representative can more effectively work on and correct one or two weaknesses.
5. Will not confuse representative with too much detail.
6. Easier for the manager to concentrate on one or two major weaknesses and remedy the underlying cause.

A good approach to the introduction of suggestions might be one of the following:
1. "Did you ever try...?"
2. "How would it have been to...?"
3. "What do you think the customer's reaction would have been if...?"
4. "Would ...have worked better if...?"

Follow-up

Once this is achieved, the manager is ready to move on to the next step in coaching... follow-up.

He must determine a specific form of follow-up to the basic contact. What are some of the methods a manager might use to follow-up on a coaching contact?

1. Check sales results for improvement.
2. Look for changes in representative's attitude.
3. Schedule subsequent coaching to ensure improvement has taken place.
4. Daily work reviews prior to or following the day's activities.
5. Discussions with representative.
6. Practise role-playing in the office (work with a tape recorder, if required).

What should a sales manager do when he/she follows-up and finds the desired improvement has not taken place?

He/she must **observe**, **evaluate** and take **appropriate action**, then **follow-up** again.

Training is a continuous, never-ending process simply because the job of helping salespersons improve themselves never ends. In planning this continuous training to increase sales volume, the sales manager needs to *plan* how to:

1. Develop a coach-player relationship between the manager and the representative.
2. Make most effective use of field coaching.
3. Motivate salespeople so they will keep developing and improving. One of the most important aspects of your work is to make salespeople *want* to learn.
4. Check the salesperson's activities, analyse their selling, and take the necessary action to raise performance standards.
5. Keep them informed on the objectives, policies, plans and programmes of the company, the division and the unit.

Every sales manager is a coach and the greater the effectiveness as a coach, the greater the effectiveness as a manager.

Real leaders are people who can get extraordinary results from ordinary people.

Self-development Report

Rep Name............   Sales Manager............   Unit #............
Date............   Calls Attempted............   Calls Completed............
Rev Generated............

Area(s) of Concentration:

1. Preparation 2. Use of Market Facts etc. 3. Recommendation 4. Time Management 5. Overcoming Objections 6. Close 7. Probing 8. Selling New Business 9. Use of Visuals in Sales 10. Presenting Benefits 11. Product Knowledge

Explanation:

Current Skill Level

Circle number indicating degree of skill

1 = weak, 4 = Average, 7 = Outstanding

Preparation	- 1 2 3 4 5 6 7 +	Recommendation	- 1 2 3 4 5 6 7 +
Approach	- 1 2 3 4 5 6 7 +	Close	- 1 2 3 4 5 6 7 +
Positioning B2B/B2C		Overcome Objections	- 1 2 3 4 5 6 7 +
Fact Finding	-1 2 3 4 5 6 7 +	Use of Aids	- 1 2 3 4 5 6 7 +
Prove Value	-1 2 3 4 5 6 7 +	Overall Rating	- 1 2 3 4 5 6 7 +
Knowledge of Product	- 1 2 3 4 5 6 7 +		

Summary

_____
_____
_____
_____
_____
_____
_____
_____
_____

Recommended course of action for representative:

_____
_____
_____
_____
_____
_____
_____

Recommended course of action for sales manager:

_____
_____
_____
_____
_____
_____
_____
_____
_____
_____
_____
_____
_____

Signature of Representative   Report Written By/Title

ooo

Effective Communication Skills

Communication, or its absence, plays an increasingly important role in our private, public and business lives. This chapter will be limited to business communications and how they can be improved to make a more effective, more profitable business organisation. An organisation's growth is dependent to a large extent on the ability of its people and departments to communicate adequately.

An adequate flow of communication moves downward, upward and sideways. A liberal definition is: "The free interchange of information, ideas and desirable attitudes between and among employees and between and among employees and management."

Effective methods of transmission involve the action of speaking or writing – the best method depends on the particular subject, its complexity, origin and destination.

We sometimes communicate by inaction. This, of course, is not generally desirable since it is vulnerable to misunderstanding. The fact that disapproval isn't voiced does not necessarily indicate approval, even though it is often interpreted in this way. A written or spoken opinion prevents that possibility.

Facial expressions, neatness, dress, nervous mannerisms and other physical actions are silent communicators. Their interpretation is likely to vary. When meeting a customer with a big smile, you wonder – did he just hear a joke or is he happy to see me? When he frowns, he is not necessarily unhappy; it may be a natural mannerism. Do you silently communicate your thoughts in this manner?

Managers who frequently rely on these nonverbal cues in their interactions with employees rarely have the trust and support of their work groups. Instead, nonverbal communications should be used to send positive messages. Some simple guidelines that will enhance the process:

- Maintain eye contact with the speaker.
- Use an open body stance, including leaning forward, which indicates an interest in what is being said.
- Use a reassuring touch on the shoulder or hand, unless the speaker finds this uncomfortable.
- Acknowledge the individual's presence promptly with a warm smile or nod of the head.
- Maintain a relaxed posture, as this communicates comfort.
- Avoid facial expressions that indicate anger, displeasure or hurriedness.
- If in an open area, walk towards the speaker to indicate interest.
- Avoid long periods of silence that may leave the impression that the listener is not concentrating on what is being said.

Be aware of gestures or other nonverbal cues that may send negative signals (e.g., finger-tapping, rolling of the eyes, shrugging of the shoulders, jiggling change and any general fidgeting).

Nonverbal communication	Signal received	Reaction from receiver
Manager looks away when talking to employee	I do not have the manager's undivided attention	Manager is too busy to listen to my problem or simply does not care
Failure to acknowledge greeting from fellow employee	This person is unfriendly	This person is unapproachable

Nonverbal communication	Signal received	Reaction from receiver
Ominous glaring (i.e., the evil eye)	This person is angry	Reciprocal anger, fear or avoidance (depending on who is sending the signal in the organisation)
Rolling of the eyes	I am not being taken seriously	This person thinks he or she is smarter or better than I am
Deep sighing	Disgust or displeasure	My opinions do not count; I must be stupid or boring to this person
Heavy breathing (sometimes accompanied by hand-wringing)	Anger or heavy stress	Avoid person at all costs
Eye contact not maintained when communicating	Suspicion and/or uncertainty	What does he/she have to hide?
Crosses arms and leans away	Apathy and closed mindedness	Person's mind is already made up; my opinion is not important
Peers over glasses	Scepticism or distrust	This person does not believe what I am saying
Continues to read while employee is speaking	Lack of interest	My opinions are not important enough to get this person's undivided attention

All ideas and information are subject to varying interpretations, the area of most frequent communication failures. A varied interpretation throughout a company or within a division results in a varied application. The result is inefficiency, lack of unity and erroneous practice. These results cost in terms of money, morale and customer or public relations.

The fact that misunderstandings do occur, errors are made and different people following the same rules do a job differently is sufficient evidence that communications do need improvement. This need is not peculiar to our business. We see it everyday in our customer's businesses as well as in our private relationships.

Quite naturally, the place to begin is at the point of origin. Good communications are purposeful and timely, related to current circumstances with fresh new methods for solutions. Much like a sales presentation, they must gain the attention and interest of the parties to whom they are directed at, show the benefits to be gained by their use and prompt the desired action and further accurate transmission of the communications.

Here are some guidelines for better communications:

1. **Make it specific:** Leave no room for unwanted interpretation. If a doubt exists, merits of the message are questioned. If it can't be specific, is it necessary?
2. **Be accurate:** Don't lend credence or authority to errors. Omission invites unfounded conclusions. Can this message be misunderstood?
3. **Speak or write forcefully:** Generate conviction and enthusiasm for the message to assure desired action. What will be the reaction to this?
4. **Keep it simple:** Present one idea at a time using examples that relate to current situations, where possible. Is this directive too complex? If so, simplify!
5. **Be direct:** Avoid hidden meanings. If your message can be understood in different ways under certain circumstances, trace the background developments leading up to the message. It isn't enough to feel you are understood – be certain you are not misunderstood. Will this be received as intended?
6. **Be discreet:** Word and example selection cannot be offensive and still permit the desired open-minded reception. Will this embarrass anyone?

We all listen to what interests us and remember what impresses us. Impressions are made through the senses of sight and hearing in our communications. In selecting the form of presentation several considerations must be made:

- *Who is the recipient of the message?*

If it is directed upward, it is probably a suggestion, a question, or a response to an earlier communication. If downward, it may be a directive, a suggestion or the relay of information.

- *Where are the recipients located?*

If the message stays in the office it will be treated differently than when transmitted over a broad area.

- *Do you meet the recipients regularly?*

If practical, you might wait for a thorough discussion.

- *What has previous experience indicated?*

It might require detailed explanation or discussion or it could be a *reminder* of previous communications.

- *Is the message complex or relatively simple?*

A complex communication will require writing and possibly discussion. If simple, conversations may be adequate.

- *What will be its reception?*

It may require face-to-face selling for justification. Resistance to change, for example, is sometimes difficult to overcome with written words.

The answers to these questions help determine whether you will write, speak or do both. If both are necessary, they will indicate whether it should be written, followed by discussion, or spoken and confirmed in writing. Obviously the different situations encountered call for different approaches, tone and choice of words. A good example of written communication followed by discussion is the designed use of sales visuals. With many points to be made the information must be written. Dialogue adds understanding and interest to move the customer towards action.

There is great advantage in spoken communication. It is the immediate knowledge of reaction and understanding. On-the-spot clarification or emphasis assures acceptance and desired action. Often, this form is not physically possible. Its use is further restricted by the nature of the message. If it is complex, part of a permanent policy or contains many instructions, it can't be transmitted except in writing. Even then, discussion is helpful. Consequently, effective communication often involves both sight and hearing. Repetition, particularly in more than one form, works for better understanding.

Since supervision is a means of getting work done through people, doesn't it follow then that improved communications with those people makes better managers, as well as improving the people that work?

A few queries a person might answer before enthusiastically accepting a message and acting on it:

1. Is it fair to all concerned?
2. Does it threaten my security?
3. Does it include my views?

4. Is it open to discussion? Are the lines of two-way communication open?
5. Does it provide for credit where this is due?
6. Does it make sound common sense?

A good check of effectiveness is the action, reaction or lack of either in response to a particular communication. Whether written or spoken, provision for feedback should be made to evaluate the degree of reception, understanding and action. This is especially valuable if the particular communication calls for a relay.

The best way to effect better communication is by example. Show the same respect for upward communications you receive as you do for those that are downward and lateral. Be certain that all are understood clearly, both as to what is expected as well as why. Questions or suggestions are more effective than commands. Follow up to see that desired actions occur. Don't overestimate the powers of retention. We retain less than one-fourth of what we hear. Ask for feedback.

Laughter can be Therapeutic

The power of laughter cannot be overlooked when communicating with co-workers and employees. It brings groups closer together and helps keep many difficult situations from getting out of hand.

Although no one should laugh at another person, laughing together is therapeutic. Work groups devoid of laughter and fun lack motivation and cohesion. This is why many corporations are training managers in laughter therapy.

Laughter and fun are suddenly the rage in the modern corporate world. Humour in the office is not difficult to achieve. It takes only time and the ability to show a genuine interest in what is happening in the workplace.

Managers should be prepared to be part of the fun by paying attention to the signals they send. These signals may tell others that the supervisor is a serious individual and feels that levity has no place at work. Managers who have a propensity for frowning and staring others down are certainly sending such signals. Remember, humour is more than telling the latest knock-knock joke; it involves approaching others with the willingness to share.

Some individuals forget this essential part of being human when they are promoted to supervisor. Laughter can make a manager's job easier because it reminds employees that he or she is human. This makes the person approachable.

Effective listening is also important in the communication process because it provides the listener with an opportunity to channel his or her responses in a meaningful manner.

Many managers unwittingly cut off employees. Their approach to communication is a sham. Most employees could and would provide more information if only they could be assured someone was really listening. But listening is more than keeping quiet when others are talking. For the supervisor, attentive listening generally means paying attention to details, understanding the picture from the employee's perspective and responding accurately and constructively.

Attentive listening is a process that begins with the listener giving the speaker his or her undivided attention. This builds rapport and indicates to the speaker that the listener values what is being said.

Other ways to listen effectively include:

- **Allow enough time:** Effective listening cannot be achieved unless the listener allocates sufficient time. Too many supervisors relegate listening to a low-priority role.

    Employees are often hurt when a supervisor tells them in words or actions, "I am in a hurry; you will have to be brief." These are times when the supervisor should schedule a meeting with the employee to complete the communication process.

- **Do not be judgmental:** One of the worst mistakes a listener can make is to go into a conversation with preconceived notions. The listener whose mind is already made up will tune out of what the speaker is saying. The attentive listener pays close attention to what is being said and does not prejudge the speaker, or his or her ideas.

- **Avoid distractions:** Listeners who are distracted easily are rarely able to respond adequately to what is being shared.

    Managers must try to remove all distractions. This includes finding a relatively quiet place for the conversation. Remove as many distractions as possible. Stay away from telephones, intercoms and the countless other irritants. Refrain from shuffling papers, gazing out of the window and so on.

- **Listen for common ground:** Employees often solve their own problems by talking them through. The manager listens for areas of agreement and addresses those first. Areas of disagreement can then be prioritised and discussed in more detail.

- **Offer encouragement:** Good listeners encourage speakers by asking questions and focusing on positive solutions.

This can be accomplished even with a negative employee by allowing the speaker sufficient time. While responding, focus on what the speaker is saying and avoid value judgments. The employee is then encouraged by the managers to talk further if he or she desires to do so. In some cases, the manager may make a referral to another source (e.g., the employee assistance programme).

- **Summarise the speaker's words:** The best way to let the speaker know how he or she is being understood is to summarise key points of the conversation.

This request for clarification assures the speaker that his or her needs will be accurately addressed. A summary also avoids any misinterpretation of information. Even the most skilled listener can misinterpret body language and voice tone. This can be prevented easily by simply asking the speaker, "What did you mean?"

Keep the Response Timely

When an employee has a problem or offers input, it is essential that the supervisor respond in a timely fashion. The manager should tell the subordinate if it would take time to provide an answer.

In some cases, this means establishing a timetable with the employee for an expected reply. A general rule is that most requests should receive a response in two days.

Employees should receive some feedback from a policy interpretation grievance within five days. The initial response in such cases may be to tell the employee that because of the nature of the concern it may take longer to resolve. This is especially true when the employee is in a grievance process that has multiple guides.

Speaking in acronyms, buzzwords and phrases is another hindrance to effective communication. Unless the listener is familiar with the terminology being used by the speaker, the conversation is meaningless and a waste of time.

It is also important to provide various options through which employees may express their opinions. Two excellent methods are regularly scheduled department meetings and face-to-face interaction with employees.

Regularly scheduled department meetings encourage employees to share opinions and promote team spirit. This is an excellent way for the supervisor to become a part of the work team and not just act the boss.

Guidelines for Responding to Employees

1. **Input:** Before announcing changes in department policy or procedures, solicit input from employees regarding the changes. Establish a timetable and methods for employees to communicate their suggestions.

2. **Employee feedback:** The supervisor should respond to employee questions and concerns within 48 hours (excluding holidays and weekends). In some instances, this may mean giving employees a time when a final decision or solution can be reached.

3. **Requested time:** The supervisor should respond no later than seven days after an employee has requested time off in advance. In some cases, employees will provide little or no advance notice. A request providing less than one week's notice should be considered individually.

4. **Recognition:** Employees should receive recognition from their immediate supervisor when a suggestion is implemented. Recognition may include issuing congratulatory citations, a letter from the supervisor or public recognition via departmental meetings or the organisation newsletter. Recognition for a job well done should be immediate to be effective.

5. **Document result of employee input:** The supervisor should monitor the results of suggestions and input received from employees. Document cost savings and other ways the input benefited the organisation. This data should then be communicated individually and in department meetings with employees. Feedback should occur no later than one week after a suggestion is made.

6. **Rejected suggestions:** The supervisor should inform the employee directly if his or her suggestion or idea is not to be implemented.

Some organisations provide suggestion programmes in an effort to increase employee input. For a suggestion programme to be effective, however, it must encourage widespread input.

The suggestion programme may be the only method through which employees can provide input directly. It is imperative to reward employees for valuable ideas that are not implemented, as well as for those that become accepted. The supervisor should explain why the suggestion or idea was rejected. An opinion survey is another excellent way to solicit input and many firms conduct them annually. While these surveys provide valuable data vital for the organisation records, the employees also accept results. Organisations that are unprepared to commit resources and time to react to the input received should avoid taking surveys.

These are some ways to solicit input from employees. But no programme can replace the importance of the supervisor making contact with the employee. The supervisor's willingness to be available to employees is still the most effective means of gaining support and, being visible, the supervisor can keep employees informed and ask for their input before major changes occur.

It takes little time and effort to be a successful communicator, yet this small investment pays more dividends than any other management skill.

The goal of all good managers should be to communicate effectively with everyone, regardless of rank or influence in the organisation. This can be achieved only if the supervisor is willing to make a commitment to the communication process.

Good communications are no accident. They are a thoughtfully applied art. They demand confidence in the source by those who receive them. This adds weight and authority, assures acceptance, action and results.

ooo

The Skills of Problem Solving

Anyone who is a failure in his personal or business life failed because of an inability to solve problems.

Problem solving is undoubtedly one of the most sought-after skills in business and industry today. Someone once said, "Don't bring me your successes, they weaken me... bring me your problems, they strengthen me." This is truly the mark of a leader. One who welcomes problems and attacks them with vigour and vitality is a true leader.

Stop and think for a minute. Do you know of a single instance where any real achievement was made in your life, or in the life of any person in history, that was not due to a problem with which the individual was faced? Everything we do in life involves problems and what determines our success is how well we approach and overcome them. Anyone who is a failure, whether in his personal or business life, probably failed because of an inability to tackle problems.

Any great personality, past or present, has only become great because of his ability to cope with and handle problems successfully. The same thing is true with companies. Each successive plateau in an organisational structure carries with it larger and more complex problems. Your progress, therefore, will be greatly determined by your ability and skill in approaching, investigating and successfully overcoming problems. This is why you, as a manager, should welcome problems. It's a gratifying experience to meet and overcome these challenges – it's also an investment in your future growth.

When confronted with a problem we can only do one of three things:

1. Let the problem get the better of us.
2. Turn our backs on the problem and hope it disappears.
3. Attack the problem knowing there is an answer – then systematically find it.

Quite obviously, the first two alternatives are ridiculous. However, they are probably the most popular. It requires very little effort to lose to a problem. And even less effort to turn your back on it. On the other hand, it takes a great deal of concentration and determination to successfully lick one problem after another.

Learning not to be afraid of problems is the first step towards solving them but problems will not solve themselves. Intelligent and systematic thinking and action is necessary.

As you know, snap judgments can produce poor decisions. Problem-solving experts say that even experience and intuition – much as they may help – can never take the place of *good, logical reasoning*. They advise this practical step-by-step approach:

1. **Define the problem:** While the real problem may seem obvious, it can be hidden or distorted by other, less important problems.

    Consider the case of a dairy company plagued by late deliveries to its customers in a particular area. At first they thought the person on that route lacked proper driving skills, but investigation revealed friction between the driver at fault and his supervisor. The real problem was not driver skills, but rather poor employee relations.

    Make sure you clearly understand the problem before you seek a solution.

2. **Assemble the facts:** Once you have clearly defined the problem, you should not rush headlong into a solution. You need all the information you can get to ensure you are heading for the right solution.

    Experts point out that much of the difficulty of problem solving comes from two sources:

    A. Not getting all the facts before making a decision.
    B. Gathering the wrong facts. Watch out against the danger of

collecting (or considering) only those facts that appear to support a preferred solution and ignoring those that point to some other remedy.

3. **List the possible solutions:** Once the facts have been assembled, they may point to more than one solution. The more choices you have, the better. The difference between a fair problem solver and a first-rate one is that the latter doesn't stop searching for solutions just because he seems to have one or two good ones.

W Clement Stone, founder of Combined Insurance, was a poor boy who began peddling newspapers on the streets of Chicago when he was six. The bigger boys tried to keep him out of their territories, so he tried selling his papers inside Hoelle's Restaurant. Stone's persistence taught him a valuable lesson: "I learned that if I couldn't solve a problem one way, I could another." Indeed, there is more than one way to solve a problem.

4. **Choose the best solution:** When you have a list of possible solutions, simply pick the solution that you think will best remedy your particular problem. Then, stick by your decision.

5. **Act on your choice:** There is no reason to hesitate once you have reached a decision for solving a problem. Act on it, there is nothing else to do.

Sometimes a solution is so simple that it gets overlooked:

A ten-year-old child was riding his bicycle when he saw traffic backed up for miles. There was a truck stuck under an overpass. The little boy asked, "What happened to the truck?"

The policemen patiently told him that the truck was stuck and the firemen were trying to get the truck out of the way so traffic could move.

The boy looked at the firemen working with their crowbars trying to free the truck. Then the little boy said: "Why don't they let the air out of the tyres?"

And that is exactly what they did! This was a simple solution that all the adult bystanders missed but one that struck the child immediately.

By systematically approaching your problems, we will by no means guarantee the right solution every time. Through this systematic approach, however, your decision will be favourable the majority of times.

It was mentioned earlier that successful people achieved their status due to their ability to handle problems. It does not mean that these people never failed. In many cases they did fail and miserably, too. But they benefited from their mistakes and never repeated their failures. The measure of success is not whether you have a tough problem to deal with but whether it's the same problem you had last year.

Edward J Vinnicombe summed it up best when he said: "It's better to make a wrong decision than no decision at all; at least you profit by the mistake. IBM's Tom Watson was asked if he was going to fire an employee who made a mistake that cost IBM $600,000. He said, 'No! I just spent $600,000 training him – why would I want somebody else to hire his experience?'"

Failure and problems should be our teacher, not our downfall. They should challenge us to new heights of accomplishment, not pull us to new depths of despair. After all, a smooth sea never made a successful sailor!

Every successful person, regardless of title, understands that business is a long road with frequent ups and downs, failures, disappointments and problems. He does not expect the going to be easy and all downhill. When he comes to a hill, he puts on more power just like he feeds more fuel when he drives his car up a gradient.

The person who knows that his success is entirely up to himself does not spend time in finding reasons why he can't do a job. Sure, he has his problems, but he never forgets that the other person has his, too. He is like a punching bag – the harder he is hit, the harder he comes back.

It is known that you can direct your thoughts, control your emotions and regulate your attitude. You can also determine whether your attitude will be positive or negative. When you meet the challenges of a problem with a positive mental attitude, you can intelligently and systematically solve each problem with which you are confronted.

Remember the time Linus from the *Peanuts* comic strip told Charlie Brown, "There's no problem too big we can't run from."

When we sigh about
Our trouble
It grows double
Everyday;

When we laugh about
Our trouble
It's a bubble
Blown away!

ooo

Delegation: A Manager's Greatest Attribute

Andrew Carnegie is quoted as stating: "The secret of success is not in doing your own work but in recognising the right person to do it."

The noun *delegation* means: *The act of empowering to act for another.* The delegation of work and duties is familiar to everyone. In fact, the executive has sometimes been described as a person who understands the art of getting other people to work for him. Yet, we find that far from being a clear-cut and simple process, delegation is, in its larger sense, a vague, overworked word. Most people believe they excel in delegation by having someone run an errand, make a simple reservation, get a car washed, etc., when they are merely assigning tasks to a subordinate.

The true art of delegation can be one of the greatest attributes of a manager. It can be a prime motivator or a prime de-motivator. Delegation actually implies relinquishing part of your responsibility and authority. By its very nature, this can be extremely difficult for most people to do. Oh, there are some of us who want someone else to share our workload, but we sometimes shudder at the thought of a subordinate knowing as much about our jobs as we do. With this attitude, we can never efficiently delegate but merely assign menial portions of our responsibility in an effort to expedite a project.

A problem with most entrepreneurs is they don't learn to let go of some of their responsibilities so that they can grow. An example is a successful entrepreneur who almost single-handedly got his company sales to $100,000 a year. When he sought venture capital to expand, the potential investors had a few questions.

"Who is your president?"

"Me."

"Who is your chief financial officer?"

"Me."

"Who is in charge of sales?"

Again the answer was, "Me."

One of the panellists asked, "How much time do you spend on sales?"

His answer, "About 10 per cent."

He was told, "You don't need money to expand. If you spend 100 per cent of your times on sales, you should quickly get to the million mark."

Many managers feel that their workload is sometimes insurmountable while others go about their daily duties and responsibilities without any apparent frustration or feeling that their work cannot be accomplished. When comparing these types of managers, we find that those who know and practise the art of delegation have more time and freedom to perform those tasks that are more meaningful and productive.

Used properly, delegation can afford many advantages, including raising time for other work and increasing the effectiveness of workers. People must recognise their efforts – they must take pride in their work and have a sense of belonging. Therefore, by using the true art of delegation, it will also serve to satisfy these needs.

There are certain dangers in delegation, however, and some of these are:

1. Rivalry can evolve in delegation if one or two members of a group are consistently sought out while others are not considered.
2. If recognition for the performance is not given, the person can become inhibited and choose to refrain from future assistance.
3. If proper explanation is not given on the reason for the assignment, some persons can fail in their assignment. In turn, this will hamper future processes.

Delegation is not a difficult art to learn. It does, however, require adherence to certain basic rules:

1. It must be a meaningful part of a job to be delegated.
2. It must be completely explained.
3. All facets of the overall job objectives should be covered.
4. Each member of a team that is sharing the objective must know the overall objective.
5. You must have complete confidence in the person's ability to perform the task delegated.
6. You must encourage questions and solicit advice and answers.
7. Periodic progress reviews must be made.
8. Expression of appreciation must be shown.

At best, delegation is an extremely complicated process because it involves the relationship between the most sensitive creatures in the world – people. Therefore, it is not something that can be done without thinking, planning and organising.

All successful leaders know how to delegate. Ross Perot, CEO of the Perot Group, said: "I surround myself with smart people and I tell them what the goal is but I never give them any kind of checklist. I say, 'Next year we are going to the moon. You're in charge.' That's how John F Kennedy approached the lunar landing. He said, 'Within ten years, we're going to put someone on the moon.' He never told anyone how to do it, but it happened anyway."

Henry Ford, on the other hand, refused to share his workload for fear of incompetent staff. Because of his strong streaks of secrecy, he was inclined to hold all the reins in his own hands. Many people feel that the Ford Motor Company dropped from a peak of 65% of the market share to only 20% because of this. Henry Ford II recognised this and immediately surrounded himself with a few people who had proved their organising and delegating skills in other firms, resulting in the transformation of Ford Motors from a slipping company to a growing company. Henry II is responsible for a much bigger industry than his grandfather was and is operating it profitably and democratically.

Finally, as one successful president commented, "We can't put a price tag on delegating, but we do pay plenty when delegating breaks down."

ooo

The Importance of Good Human Relations

Listen to this conversation between the wind and the sun. The wind said, "See how easily I can blow away the coat from that man below."

So the wind blew up a storm. But the stronger the wind blew, the more the man clutched the coat, holding it tight around him. Then it was the sun's turn. With a smile, the sun beamed its warming rays down until the man took off his coat voluntarily. In much the same way, human relations means getting things done in a positive way.

Behaviour between individuals and among members of a group is evidence of the relationship that exists. Like communications, these human relationships are continuous and beamed in all directions – up, down and sideways. They are both subject to guidance and control.

However, while efficient communications are a casual factor designed to produce a desired result, good human relations are an effect. They are the result of many factors, including efficient communications.

To direct several individual members of a group to function as a team requires establishing a high degree of compatibility. It requires respect for authority and for one another. Before this can be accomplished, it is necessary to recognise the causes of incompatibility and the environment in which compatibility will grow. It is dangerous to attempt to change behaviour without understanding the causes of that behaviour.

Each person in a group is an individual with individual characteristics. Generally, these are grouped as social, psychological and physical characteristics. Each individual has different beliefs, desires and economic needs. No two people possess the same characteristics and needs. Consequently, in laying the groundwork for optimum compatibility, it is necessary to consider and satisfy the individual requirements before proceeding with those of the group.

Since a manager's success is dependent on that of his group, 'The Golden Rule' (*do unto others as you would wish them to do unto you*) is especially appropriate in this endeavour. A manager learns to know the people in his group – their habits, strong points, weaknesses and private lives, as well as where he stands in their eyes. Without this knowledge, he isn't able to direct the group to maximum potential. However, over-familiarity can be as detrimental as lack of knowledge of the men as individuals.

Managers must earn the respect of their people. Instant respect is not bestowed on a person when he or she is given the title 'Manager'. The group depends on you as their manager for leadership, praise, direction and support. If the individuals in the group like and respect you, they will tend to identify with you. This process of identifying with others is going on all around us. We identify with our boss or someone else whom we admire and respect. In any group there is usually a leader – someone to whom the others can look up to. If your people find it possible to identify with you, then you will be accepted by them as the leader. If this personal identification is impossible, someone else will wear the unofficial mantle of leadership. You will have a difficult time carrying out your job as manager if this happens.

In striving to stay on good terms with their people, managers often make the mistake of leaning too far in the direction of the employee. The close day-to-day working relationship with their people and the desire to be liked by their employees tends to make some managers forget their responsibilities as part of the management team. It robs them of the authority they must maintain. It permits favouritism – real or imaginary – to enter the group unit and allows personality clashes to arise. Imagine morale and productivity in a group where some of these things have occurred.

By fulfilling responsibilities to our managers and by insisting that those whom we supervise do the same, we keep the reality of the work situation clearly in focus for all concerned.

Predictable, fair and equal treatment goes a long way towards good human relationships. Applied to all phases of unit activity from territory assignments to asking for assistance or delegating responsibility, the known fact that the manager's decision will be fair precludes any rumbling of favouritism.

Managing a sales unit requires that the manager be somewhat of a lay psychologist. Those who are experts in human relations use division to prevent collision of personality. Having recognised a potential clash, it can be avoided by injecting another member's personality as a buffer. After a short time, the reasons for the incompatibility will be lost.

Recognition for a job well done is a basic ingredient for good human relations. We all protect and defend our ego to the extent that recognition is ranked right behind financial reward and ahead of many side benefits in most motivation studies. While recognition should be public for great benefits, on the opposite side of the coin, criticism or discipline should be private. Planned recognition and discipline, with group compatibility in mind, will de-emphasise some causes of personality clashes.

While many know General Douglas McArthur, few know that he was not only a great general but also very adept at human relations. He once had the idea of writing a report of every visiting dignitary's background and interest. The next time the dignitary returned McArthur was able to make the visitor feel important and flattered by all that he remembered about him!

Most importantly, human relations mean caring about your people. Charles Percy was made president of Bell & Howell before he was 40 years old. Fascinated by his rise, a reporter asked many people as to what they attributed Percy's success. The answer always was: "From the very beginning, he showed a knack for being able to get the most out of other people."

Sensitivity to the needs and desires of other people ultimately leads to success.

ooo

Self-development

This lesson will give you guidance in planning your own development as a front-line sales manager, as a leader of men, as a potential higher echelon executive. It will touch on those things you can do for yourself as a manager, whether or not the company you work for happens to have a formal executive development programme. The principles of self-development apply in either case.

The Nature of Development

Growth on the job is one of the important needs that must be filled if a salesman is to remain happy in selling. He must feel that he is getting better; he must have a sense of progress. And the very same need exists in all men in any job, including with you in your job. Development, then, is something that is desirable for its own sake. It makes your job exciting and satisfying.

Development has other real benefits as well. Two meanings of the word *develop* are: *to unfold more completely, to form or expand by a process of growth*. The "unfolding" process inherent in development suggests a "bringing out" of something that is already there. Some flowers, for instance, close up at night, folding their petals inward. With the morning sun, the petals unfold once more, revealing the flower in full bloom.

Most sales managers are, to some degree, like a flower that has closed in on itself – they have much of the knowledge and many of the skills they need to do an outstanding job, but they ignore much of what they know and fail to exercise the management skills they possess. Often it takes the "sun" of a development programme to get the manager to blossom – to realise or make full use of the ability he already has.

So development, on the one hand, is aimed at helping the manager put to use information and skills he already possesses; on the other hand, it is intended to expand his knowledge, teach him new skills, or increase his present skill. In one case, development is a matter of making better use of existing talents; in the other, it is a matter of creating new talents.

Thus, development in the unfolding sense is concerned almost entirely with a manager's present job, while development in the expanding sense deals with both the present job and with grooming for a higher position in management.

Steps in the Self-development Process

Experience is still the best teacher. Most managers will develop into better managers just by managing. They will learn, often painfully, that they should do some things and not others. Thus, to some extent, development "takes care of itself".

But no front-line sales manager can expect experience alone to make him a fully effective leader and administrator. Successful sales managers will be those who give thought to their growth, who plan for it and who work hard at it.

The process of self-development involves some basic steps:

1. **Identifying Development Needs.** By this point in the course, the importance of goal setting should be obvious to you. Having specific objectives is just as important in constructing a self-development programme as it is in setting up a sales training programme, conducting a meeting, or holding a coaching session. How you go about deciding what areas your development programme should cover will be discussed in the section on *Making a Self-appraisal*.

2. **Choosing Methods.** Once you decide what improvements you want to make in yourself, you must choose the way or ways of effecting these improvements. Often, no choice exists. For example, if your self-appraisal discloses that you are doing something well enough but not often enough (e.g., field coaching), your only choice is to do more of it.

   However, in other cases, there may be several methods you might use to make the necessary improvement. If you are a poor leader of meetings, for instance, you might choose to read some books on the subject (and follow their advice), or take a public-speaking course, or become active in an organisation where you can get experience in committee leadership, or practise your "fixed" portion of all meetings you hold more intensely. Or you might do all these things if time and circumstances permit. The more ways there are to correct a weakness or build a skill, the better chance you have of being successful in meeting your objective.

3. **Scheduling the Programme.** Good intentions win no battles. It is not enough to be aware of a weakness; it is not enough to have a plan for overcoming the weakness – you must have the determination and self-discipline to go through with it. Target dates should be marked on your calendar and your own progress evaluated regularly. The feeling of accomplishment that comes from completing a self-administered programme of self-improvement can alone be sufficient reward for undertaking that programme.

What was the most recent activity you undertook on your own initiative that could be considered developmental?

_____
_____
_____
_____
_____

Making a Self-appraisal

Diagnosis must always precede treatment, whether the individual involved is a doctor examining a sick patient, a plumber confronted with a clogged drain, a social worker handling a delinquent child, or a sales manager bent on improving himself. This means you must look carefully at your job and at the effectiveness with which you fill it. And, if you intend to move up the management ladder, it means you must look at the requirements needed to fill higher positions and look at yourself to see how you need to improve in order to qualify for such responsibilities. Suggestions for getting an objective look at yourself follow.

Writing Your Own Job Description

As far as your development is concerned, your first and most important concern should be with your present job. If you are successful where you are, you stand a good chance of moving up. (This is not to suggest that you shouldn't set your sights high and work hard to get there.) A man who is preoccupied with tomorrow too often makes mistakes today, ruining any chance he has for advancement. Your handling of your present assignment is the best possible yardstick for measuring your ability to take on a bigger one.

Since success on your present job is critical, it is obvious that you must know exactly what your present job is. Unfortunately, front-line sales manager are often less aware of their responsibilities than they think they are. Some companies prepare complete job descriptions for their sales managers, outlining in some detail the specific duties and responsibilities of their job. Such guides are invaluable aids to self-appraisal by the manager inasmuch as they can serve as a checklist he can use to see what he does well and what he needs to improve upon. This comparison of job expectations with performance is the first step in self-development.

This is your assignment for this lesson. After making your first draft, copy it on the Assignment Sheet provided. List, as concisely as possible and in approximate order of importance as judged by you, the 10 most important duties or responsibilities of your job. Be as specific as possible. (For instance, "**1.** To recruit, hire and train new salesmen of sufficient quality and quantity to keep my group up to full strength of eight men. **2.** To keep all men in my group up-to-date on all new products, both as to what they are and how they can be sold through monthly meetings, special training sessions, bulletins, memos, and personal conversation.") When constructing this job description, try to answer the questions: Who? What? When? Where? Why? How?

Analysing Your Strengths and Weaknesses

By thoughtfully going over your job description, you should be able to spot areas of your performance that could improve. Of course, you have to be tough-minded almost to the extreme about your self-analysis, or very little good will come of it.

The self-questioning technique is the best method for conducting an audit of your managerial skills, habits and attitudes. For example, if field coaching is one of the important duties you listed (as it almost certainly should be), you should ask yourself pertinent questions about your coaching technique, using as a guide not only your own knowledge of what you should do, but other sources as well – perhaps a company directive, or a book on the subject. This reference to outside sources not only reminds you of things you already know but may not be doing, they also teach you new things. Thus, they aid growth in your job as well as help you "unfold".

If your self-questioning reveals things that you know how to do but aren't doing regularly enough, you should make a note of it. Some managers keep self-reminders in their desks or tacked on their walls that they refer to regularly. Simple notes such as "Make personal contact with each salesman at least once a week" or "What have you done today for the men in the field?" have proven to be invaluable aids to managers intent on improving their supervisory skills. Such reminders aid the "unfolding" process involved in development.

If a weakness that requires more elaborate plans for improvement is uncovered, you can jot your development plans down on a sheet of paper (it always pays to write down any programme you set up for yourself), such as setting up objectives, specific activities you will undertake, dates for accomplishing certain tasks, etc. Then you can transfer your plans to your calendar or have a secretary set up a call-up file for that programme.

Incidentally, it helps to mention your programme to someone – perhaps your wife – who will be interested in hearing how it is coming along. Having mentioned your plans once, you will be reluctant to back out for fear of losing face. Sharing your plans, and maybe even bragging a bit, commits you publicly to your development programme.

What follow are the kinds of questions you might ask yourself that relate to certain front-line sales management tasks. Your answers may point to an area for development. These questions do not exhaust any of the subjects covered. They are simply intended to show the kind of self-questioning you should engage in during self-appraisal.

Coaching

- Do I maintain continuity between one coaching session and the next?
- Do I work in the field only when a salesman is in trouble, thus giving the impression that coaching is an emergency measure?
- Do I give each man the field coaching he needs?
- Do I familiarise myself with a salesman's record before every coaching session?
- During joint calls conducted for coaching, do I always wait to see what the salesman will do of his own accord without my intervention?
- After coaching a salesman in the field, do I sit down with him and systematically go over the weaknesses I observed, and give him practical suggestions about what he can do to correct these weaknesses?

Order Giving

- Do I give orders forcefully and without apology?
- In giving an order do I always explain specifically what I expect to be achieved by its execution?
- Do I tailor the wording and timing of my orders to the nature of the salesman to whom it is given?
- Do I always check to verify that the salesman has fully understood the order?
- Before giving important orders, do I always determine exactly what it is I want the order to accomplish?
- Do I tell the salesman by what standards his execution of the order will be measured, and how and when this measurement will be made?

Criticising and Correcting

- Do I always have the courage to make complete criticism even though it may be unpleasant?

- When necessary, do I administer criticism of a salesman with specific instructions for corrective action?
- Before criticising a salesman, do I always ask myself, "Am I going to contribute to his development in some useful way?"
- Do I avoid comparing a salesman unfavourably with a colleague?
- Do I base my criticism on some aspects of the man's performance, rather than on his personality, intelligence, or character?
- Do I try to make an effort to have the salesman himself analyse the situation and, in effect, self-criticise?
- Do I always present the benefits the man will receive from the corrective action I want?

Appraising and Evaluating Salesmen
- When evaluating a salesman, do I remain as performance-oriented as possible, confining myself to an objective analysis of numerical or readily observable data?
- In pointing out to a salesman what he can do to improve his performance, am I careful to document the benefits he will receive from this improvement?
- Am I always detailed and specific in the things I tell the salesman he can do to gain the knowledge, skills and habits he needs to improve his performance?
- Do I provide the sustained direction and help, including field coaching, a salesman needs to achieve the objectives of his development programme?
- Do I carefully observe the salesman's progress, making appropriate comments concerning his progress?

Training
- Do I have a long-term and continuous programme for my salesman, one that is carefully integrated into company-wide training activities?
- Have I organised the subject matter of my training programme according to the six broad areas – company knowledge, technical knowledge, market knowledge, skills, habits and attitudes – and determined the materials and methods I am going to use to cover each area?
- Am I maintaining an organised sales-training resource file of booklets, magazine articles, memos, sales bulletins, books, etc., relating to a subject I might want to cover in a training session?

- Whenever possible, do I employ visual aids when training my salesman, using "homemade" charts and other materials?
- Do I schedule my training sessions so that the total time available is allocated in an efficient manner, and related subjects are grouped together, one session picking up where another left off?
- Have I established objectives for my training so that I can judge its effectiveness?

Sales Meetings

- In planning sales meetings, do I have an objective that merits a meeting?
- Do I construct a written agenda of the points I want the meeting to cover, the order in which they will be presented, and the approximate amount of time to be devoted to each?
- Before a meeting, do I rehearse what I am going to say, and practise using the charts and any other visual aids I intend to employ?
- Do I prepare my salesman for sales meetings by giving them advance written notice and, whenever feasible, a brief outline of the meeting?
- If a salesman is to conduct part of the meeting, do I give him a detailed assignment well in advance of the meeting and go over his role with him a day or two before the meeting?
- Do my men participate to the utmost in sales meetings through controlled discussions, practise selling and similar contributions?

Motivating and Stimulating Salesmen

- Do I recognise that motivating salesmen involves no tricks or attempts at manipulation, but rather consists of a continuous and long-term effort to provide the guidance, control and support needed to create a healthy work climate?
- Am I continually conscious of my salesman's job-related needs – the satisfaction they seek from their work – and do I do what I can to see that their work fulfils these needs?
- Am I interested in my salesmen as individuals, and am I alert for opportunities to demonstrate this interest to them?
- Do I foster healthy competition between my salesmen?
- Am I aware that salesmen prize non-financial rewards, but are typically reluctant to admit it?

Maintaining Control

- Do I have a clear idea of the objectives my salesmen should seek and the activities they have to undertake to attain those goals?
- Do my salesmen understand their objective and the activities needed to attain them?
- Do I consistently check my salesmen's reports, measure the degree to which they have fulfilled specific assignments and directives, and observe other evidence of their activity?
- Do my salesmen know that I am going to know what they did or failed to do?
- Am I quick to correct and re-direct salesmen when my observation of their performance indicates that such correction and re-direction is necessary?

Getting the Opinion of Your Superior

No man can ever be completely objective about himself. Thus, as you go about the task of self-appraisal, you should seek the opinions of others about your work. And perhaps the man who can help you the most is your immediate superior. If your company has a programme of periodic appraisal of front-line sales managers, then you have a head start on your development programme. However, if no such appraisal programme exists, you can still get some helpful opinions, observations, and ideas from your boss.

Unfortunately, probably no employee is more widely separated from his immediate superior than the front-line sales manager. The gap is usually even greater than that existing between the salesman and his manager. Your superior probably has little opportunity to see you in day-to-day action. He may visit your office from time to time, but the extent of his contact with you is probably limited. This means that the help he can give you will depend largely on what you are able to tell him about your problems and your development needs. There are few executives who would not be pleased by an employee who comes to him for help on a self-development programme. (Showing this sign of initiative is in itself a good thing.) Your approach can be quite informal. Simply ask for an opportunity to discuss your work. Ask for any opinion he might have, point out areas where you have had difficulty and ask for guidance, get his ideas about what methods of development would best suit your particular needs.

Of course, you should not overdo requests for your superior's help or appraisal. Limit such conversations to times when you have something truly important to discuss.

Choose one area of your sales management activities (from the 10 you listed on your "job description") that you feel you handle less effectively than you would like. Copy it below. Then make a note on your calendar to ask your boss for some ideas on how you might improve your performance in that area.

_____
_____
_____
_____

Learning About Yourself Through Your Salesmen

You can learn as much about yourself by making a good appraisal of one of your men as you learn about him. If a salesman has insufficient product knowledge, chances are that you have failed in your training of him. If he does not do what you want him to, you have insufficient control. In other words, your salesmen tend to mirror your weakness as a superior, and all you sometimes need to do to make an appraisal of yourself as a superior is read that reflection of yourself.

It is not an easy thing for a leader to accept responsibility for the weakness of his subordinates, but that is one of the burdens of management. The fault for a salesman's shortcomings may not always lie with his immediate manager, but often it does, and the responsibility for these faults is the manager's – that fact is inescapable.

The very fact that salesmen tend to style themselves after their manager makes their conduct a good guide to your own. Attitudes are particularly contagious, and any sign of a poor attitude such as discouragement, disrespect for the company, laziness, ill-manners, or fear should at least prompt you to look at yourself to see if you have, in any way, passed this attitude along to the salesman who is suffering from it.

Without writing out names, identify what you feel to be the greatest weakness of each of your salesmen. Briefly mention how you might, through better leadership, correct this weakness. (E.g., "X is unwilling to work hard – he needs more challenge, prodding and criticism, and more direct day-to-day control".)

_____
_____
_____
_____

Creating Your Development Programme

It is one thing to know what your weaknesses are and the areas in which you need to develop, and quite another to do something about them. Although it takes a good man to admit his own faults, it takes an even better one to correct them.

Your development "programme" need not be elaborate. As has already been suggested, just by keeping a reminder list of things you must do more frequently (or of areas in which you must improve) can act as an invaluable aid to your development – if you keep the list always in your mind.

Strengthening Job-related Skills

Strengthening job-related skills such as coaching, order giving, training, and counselling is often simply a matter of will and practise on your part. It seems to be human nature that we do those things that we like to do and can do well and avoid doing those things that we don't like to do and don't do well. Thus, a manager who hates to coach or who doesn't do it well (the two traits often go hand-in-hand) may avoid coaching, if possible. What he needs to develop is the will to improve his coaching technique and practise on it. He must force himself to get out in the field with his men on a regular basis. In these visits, he must make a conscious effort to follow all the accepted rules of good coaching, which he will have in mind because he honed up on the subject beforehand.

In cases where you lack the skills required on the job (rather than simply being deficient or disliking to perform a certain task), will and practise alone may not be sufficient. For example, if you find yourself lacking confidence and composure during sales meetings, no matter how many such meetings you have held, it may not help you much. If so, you may want to enrol in a public-speaking course, where your confidence is built up not so much from doing something, as from the knowledge that you are doing it correctly.

It has already been mentioned that your immediate superior may have some good suggestions about ways in which you can develop certain skills you feel need sharpening. Others can be of help too – fellow managers, business associates, friends or professors you had in college, etc. They may remind you of principles that you had forgotten or suggest a good book on a particular subject. Sometimes, a man can become defeatist about his ability to improve or develop. He will feel that there is nothing he can do that he hasn't already tried. But fight this feeling. Very often, your boss or others can come up with a good idea that you never dreamed of.

Describe a job-related weakness you think you have that you have not done much about because you felt there was very little that could be done about it.

_____
_____
_____
_____

There are other things you can do to increase your job-related knowledge and skill. The local sales executives' club provides an excellent opportunity for the front-line sales manager to exchange ideas with his fellow managers. Many of the skills you need to manage your men effectively can be further developed if you become a truly active member in a sales executives' club. You could even join some local service organisation such as the Rotary or Lions Club or a professional or industrial society related to your job. Committee leadership or office holding, for example, provides excellent practise in the art of getting people to cooperate with each other and to work for you.

Books and magazines directly related to the management of salesmen are plentiful, and can greatly aid your development on the job. Less directly related reading, but no less helpful, can be found in books and periodicals on such subjects as leadership, personnel management, supervision, human relations, and administration. Almost all successful sales managers are engaged in a continuous programme of carefully selected reading in areas related to their job. Perhaps your local librarian can suggest books for you to read.

Your fellow managers are one of the best sources of ideas about what reading material is worthwhile. They can alert you to particularly good books, articles, or magazines. Many sales managers have a small library that they are willing to share, as perhaps you do.

Sometimes, development opportunities come at unexpected times. One manager, for instance, was asked to teach salesmanship to an adult night school class. He found what he had put into his preparation made him a far better trainer of his men. Still another manager found that his involvement in a local political campaign gave him greater insight into the feelings of his salesmen.

Being Your Own "Tough Boss"

The distance and infrequent contact that exists between the typical front-line manager and his immediate superior has already been mentioned. This means that you are on your own to a much greater degree than supervisors of almost any other type. You are, to a large extent, your own boss and, because of this fact, you are largely responsible for your day-to-day discipline and control. Since it is through such discipline and control that so much of the development that takes place on a job occurs, it is important that you learn to be a "tough boss" for yourself.

You might get a better idea of what being your own tough boss involves if you imagine how you would behave if your own boss were constantly sitting outside your office, watching you at work, listening to your conversations, or if he were accompanying you on every one of your trips to the field! The behaviour you would exhibit under those circumstances should be that which you should always exhibit. If it is, then you are a good self-manager.

Typical items that might be added to a list of things that a tough boss would insist you do, but that you might be tempted to put off or ignore if he weren't around, include:

- Working hard without watching the clock.
- Getting to work promptly.
- Never over-staying at lunchtime.
- Working until the job is finished.
- Doing important things that you dislike doing.
- Accepting full responsibility for your men's performance and development.
- Criticising your men when necessary.
- Keeping your deskwork up-to-date.

The reason these seemingly little things are important in your development is twofold. In the first place, if you stick to your job, and if you do those things you don't really like to do, you are certain to become a better manager. Secondly, the self-discipline required to be your own tough boss is the kind of discipline you will need if you are to move up the sales management ladder.

Recall to yourself one "little" thing that you allow yourself to get away with that you know you would not try if you use the tough boss test.

Planning Your Upward Progress

Although growth (and "unfolding") in your present job is the most important aspect of your development, you should make some effort to grow towards better things as well – you should prepare yourself for new duties and greater responsibilities so that you are ready to assume them should you be asked to do so.

Many of the skills and attitudes that make you a successful front-line sales manager are the same skills and attitudes that make your boss successful, and that make his boss successful, and so on up the ladder. But there are differences as well. Higher positions require a somewhat broader point-of-view. The knowledge required is usually more refined, more technical, and often more theoretical. For example, the front-line sales manager is more concerned with selling, while his superiors are more concerned with marketing. Or, where you might have to understand thoroughly the compensation plan for your salesmen, you would probably not be expected to have the knowledge needed to redesign the plan; but a senior sales executive might be expected to do this.

Here are some of the areas in which most front-line sales managers would probably have to become more proficient or knowledgeable if they hoped to move up to higher sales management:

Administration. The "science" of administration is much talked-about these days. The sales executive who does not have some knowledge of the principles of organisation – involving such concepts as span of control, line and staff functions, and accountability vs. responsibility – will be at a disadvantage in a business community where these principles are discussed and used everyday. Of course, the structure of an organisation is not the only concern of management – the people who man the structure are just as important. Thus, knowledge of personnel administration is also important to the sales executive. This field, broadly speaking, would include subjects like human relations and communications, as well as the subjects that are the traditional concern of the personnel administrator.

Accounting. Top executives are almost invariably good fact and figure men. They know where to get the facts they need and they know how to interpret them. Accounting, as used here, involves the wide area of cost control, profit centres, finance – in other words, it goes beyond the bookkeeping sense of the term. Familiarity with the world of accounting – in both its big and little sense – is invaluable to the high-level sales executive.

Economics. Since the success of an individual company within our economic society is tied ultimately to the success of the economy as a whole, an understanding of the principles of economics is important to any executive. Such matters like business cycles, credit, influence of government and the growth of new markets are all a legitimate concern of an upper echelon sales executive.

Production. The problems inherent in manufacturing should be of interest to any sales executive in a company that sells a manufactured product. Often, the engineering and sales departments are at odds because they do not understand one another's problems. To provide sound marketing guidance, the well-versed sales executive should know what his plant can and cannot do; what special technical capabilities it has; its capacity for expansion; its limitation etc.

Marketing. It was suggested earlier that marketing was different from selling. A top sales executive must have knowledge that a front-line manager need not bother about. The wider field of marketing involves objectives like pricing, advertising, market research, product development, distribution, packaging, competitive strategy, and the legal questions involved in government regulation.

You probably already have much of the advanced knowledge you need should you be promoted. You may also be aware of the weakness in your training, experience and education. Most gaps can be filled through intelligent reading and distance study programmes. Indeed, some of the lessons that follow in this course are designed to help you gain the broader knowledge and vision that is required to advance up the management ladder.

Now, note down your greatest gaps in the knowledge you'd need if you were promoted to a higher sales management position:

_____
_____
_____
_____

Further Guidelines for Development

All development is not directly related to performance in your day-to-day job or to performance in some higher, yet-to-be reached position. Although you are a manager, you are also a man, and it is impossible to separate the kind of man you are from the kind of manager you are.

The following guidelines for development are concerned primarily with your development as a person, although they necessarily touch on your job as well.

Pattern yourself after some noteworthy superior. Almost any successful man can point to some person in his life after whom he modelled himself. Perhaps you already have someone whose polished manner and behaviour you admire and copy. This person may or may not be an immediate superior; he may not even be with your company. But that you have such a model is important, for more of your successful behaviour than you realise can be attributed to the identification you make with successful people.

Guard your health. "A man without his health has nothing." Unfortunately, the truth of this statement dawns on most people only after they have become ill or have ruined their health. The importance of things like sleep, exercise, a good diet, moderation in both food and drink, and healthy diversions are stressed so much these days that perhaps the advice falls on deaf ears. Young men are particularly apt to feel that they can go "wide open" all the time without strain. But the toll is being exacted silently, whether the man realises it or not.

Any front-line sales manager interested in doing the best possible job where he is, with an eye towards better things, owes it to himself and to his company to take care to guard his health. This care should include at least an annual physical check-up. And don't put off having a doctor look at you if you sense that something is wrong. Some men, either because they dislike pampering themselves or because they are afraid, delay or put off entirely an examination that could save them great problems later.

Broaden your horizon. The advice, "broaden your horizon", has become a cliché, but its validity is unquestionable. It is the man with wide-ranging interests who usually succeeds – he is not a specialist in the narrow sense, he finds interest and value in almost every aspect of life. He develops associations with people who can enrich his life. He has not lost his curiosity, his interest in the "new". His enthusiasm for life is strong. His hobbies and outside interests often have nothing to do with his livelihood, but they can make him more effective in it.

The successful man sees the relationship between diverse things; for example, he understands and appreciates the fact that by reading a book on anthropology, he undoubtedly will learn something that he can apply to his job – and even if this doesn't happen, that fact will not deter him from reading the book, because he knows that the sheer act of learning and discovery will enrich his imagination and strengthen his mind. He becomes a better man and, with it, a better manager.

Finally, that's what this book is all about.

ooo

Afterword

Well done! Congratulations and thanks for taking the time to read *Bite-sized bits on Common-sense Management*. Now I'd like to turn the tables by asking you to do me a favour. Let's make it your turn to write now. What topics did you like best that seemed most relevant to you? And what were the least relevant ones? What would you like to learn more about? What ideas do you have that could be included in future writings or training sessions?

Hope to see you some day. If we can help in some way, do let us know... it's your turn to write now!

Gerard Assey F Inst SMM (UK)

Chief Executive

Collection Skills

37/11 Siva Shanmugham Street

Nungambakkam

Chennai – 600 034

INDIA

Email: gerard@collectionskills.com

www.ingramcontent.com/pod-product-compliance
Lightning Source LLC
Chambersburg PA
CBHW080553230426
43663CB00015B/2827